New Insights on Covered Call Writing

Also available from
Bloomberg Press

Investing Under Fire:
Winning Strategies from the Masters
for Bulls, Bears, and the Bewildered
Edited by Alan R. Ackerman
(June 2003)

New Thinking in Technical Analysis:
Trading Models from the Masters
Edited by Rick Bensignor

Profit in the Futures Markets!:
Insights and Strategies for Futures and
Futures Options Trading
by Jake Bernstein

Tom Dorsey's Trading Tips:
A Playbook for Stock Market Success
by Thomas J. Dorsey and the DWA Analysts

Wall Street Secrets for Tax-Efficient Investing:
From Tax Pain to Investment Gain
by Robert N. Gordon with Jan M. Rosen

Investing in Hedge Funds:
Strategies for the New Marketplace
by Joseph G. Nicholas

A complete list of our titles is available at
www.bloomberg.com/books

New Insights on Covered Call Writing

The Powerful Technique That Enhances Return
and Lowers Risk in Stock Investing

RICHARD LEHMAN
LAWRENCE G. MCMILLAN

Bloomberg Press
Princeton, New Jersey

Books are available for bulk purchases at special discounts. Special editions or book excerpts can also be created to specifications. For information, please write: Special Markets Department, Bloomberg Press.

BLOOMBERG, BLOOMBERG NEWS, BLOOMBERG FINANCIAL MARKETS, OPEN BLOOMBERG, THE BLOOMBERG FORUM, COMPANY CONNECTION, COMPANY CONNEX, BLOOMBERG PRESS, BLOOMBERG PROFESSIONAL LIBRARY, BLOOMBERG PERSONAL BOOKSHELF, and BLOOMBERG SMALL BUSINESS are trademarks and service marks of Bloomberg L.P. All rights reserved.

This publication contains the authors' opinions and is designed to provide accurate and authoritative information. It is sold with the understanding that the authors, publisher, and Bloomberg L.P. are not engaged in rendering legal, accounting, investment-planning, or other professional advice. The reader should seek the services of a qualified professional for such advice; the authors, publisher, and Bloomberg L.P. cannot be held responsible for any loss incurred as a result of specific investments or planning decisions made by the reader.

First edition published 2003
1 3 5 7 9 10 8 6 4 2

Library of Congress Cataloging-in-Publication Data

Lehman, Richard
    New insights on covered call writing : the powerful technique that enhances return and lowers risk in stock investing / Richard Lehman and Lawrence G. McMillan.
        p. cm.
Includes index.
    ISBN 1-57660-133-1 (alk. paper)
    1. Stock options. 2. Investments. I. McMillan, Lawrence G. II. Title

HG6042 .L44 2003
332.63'228--dc21   2002155816

Acquired by Kathleen A. Peterson
Edited by Elizabeth Ungar

This book is dedicated to the memory of Thomas Farrell (1950–2002), whose untimely passing prevented him from seeing the completion of the work he so strongly supported.

Contents

BUILDING THE FOUNDATION

Part II

EXECUTING THE STRATEGY

Acknowledgments

THE AUTHORS WISH TO ACKNOWLEDGE THE FOLLOWING FOR THEIR assistance:

Matthew Moran, Marty Kearney, and Debra Peters at the CBOE
Mark Johnson at TD Securities on the Floor of the CBOE
Greg Stevens at The Options Institute
Ernie Zerenner at PowerOptions
John Brasher at CallWriter.com
Richard J. Shapiro at Ernst & Young LLP

With special thanks to Fred Gruber of AppreCap Services for the extensive amount of time he spent reviewing the material.

Preface

COVERED CALL WRITING IS PERHAPS THE MOST WIDELY ACCESSIble option strategy. It can be utilized by any stock owner and does not require huge minimums, margin accounts, or advanced theoretical analysis. It can be practiced in a retirement account as well as in investment or speculative accounts. However, in the universe of all stock owners, it is a strategy that to date, at least, has been practiced by only a devoted few. For this reason alone, it is appropriate to have an entire book written on the topic.

There are plenty of other reasons as well, though, why *New Insights on Covered Call Writing: The Powerful Technique That Enhances Return and Lowers Risk in Stock Investing* is both timely and an invaluable resource for investors. First and foremost is the fact that covered writing will outperform stock ownership in any market except a strongly rising one. The investment landscape that we can expect over the next several years will quite likely be ideal for covered call writing. While there are likely to be some periods of strongly rising stock prices in the coming years, it is this writer's opinion that the market will suffer through a series of declines, punctuated by mini-recoveries, much as was seen in the time period between 1966 and 1974. In fact, the *entire* sixteen-year period between 1966 and 1982 can be considered one of struggling stock prices. If history repeats itself (which it never does exactly, of course), stock prices may have made little or no headway by the year 2016, since the market's peak in 2000. However, a strategy that includes selling option premium over that length of time would surely produce returns superior to those of merely owning stocks.

Note that this is not to say that covered writing will make money in all markets. There is considerable downside risk in the strategy, but that risk is *less* than the risk of owning stock outright. So, it is correct to say that covered call writing will outperform plain-vanilla stock ownership during a period of declining stock prices.

With the availability of some 2,300 stocks on which listed options can be written, just about every stock owner can avail himself of this strategy, from the smallest individual investor to the largest institutional money manager.

In addition to having options available on so many stocks, the covered writer of today has a much easier time gathering pertinent information about the strategy, from arithmetical returns to more complex analyses involved in calculating and predicting volatility. The Internet is one big reason why. There are websites that provide data and mathematical calculations that quickly and accurately compute pertinent results—results that, in the past, would have been much more arduous to obtain. These numbers, generally related to the returns and protection that the strategy can offer the stock owner, are the backbone of how the strategy is implemented.

Covered writing also reduces the volatility of one's portfolio. Volatility is not a difficult or arcane concept. It is merely a measure of how fast a stock changes in price, or in a broader sense, how fast the *market* changes in price. Saying that covered call writing reduces the volatility of a portfolio means that the strategy will lose less money in bear markets and make less in bull markets than outright stock ownership will. However, there is empirical evidence that, over the long run, a portfolio of covered call writing can produce returns commensurate with buying and holding stock. If these returns can be achieved with less volatility, that is clearly another advantage of covered call writing.

As you may know, or as you will certainly learn in reading this book, covered call writing is even more advantageous when options are expensive. This happens when the overall stock market is volatile. Beginning in 1996, overall volatility increased dramatically. During the bear market that began in 2000, volatility has increased even more. This means that covered call writers can take in more premium, whether they are selling short-term (one- or two-month) options or longer-term LEAPS options. More premium provides more downside protection, which of course may be sorely needed if stocks are volatile during a declining market.

It is again this writer's opinion that volatility will remain high in the market, not necessarily for as long as sixteen years, but as long as investors are nervous about their stock holdings. That could be for a considerable length of time, or for several more years, at least. If we experience a series of bull and bear markets in the future, prices are likely to remain volatile.

Looking at the historical record, in the period between 1966 and 1974, three dismal bear markets and two booming bull markets occurred, and each was considerable in magnitude. In other words, prices were volatile. Between 1974 and 1982, prices were less volatile, with the market trading in a narrower range over those years. As has been noted, history never exactly repeats itself, yet it seems likely that we will undergo several years of volatile prices, as the last excesses of the huge bull market of the 1980s and 1990s are expunged, and then perhaps enjoy a period of tranquility as a base is built before the next great bull market takes place. Covered call writing will be an ideal strategy for many during that time period.

Because many market experts foresee a period of high volatility and struggling stock prices, this strategy is favorably viewed and increasingly practiced by professionals in the field of portfolio management. However, the average investor can *just as readily* take advantage of this strategy. The necessary data is both available and easily within reach, and the specific instructions for implementation are contained in this book. One of the real advantages of covered writing is that it generally can be understood by any stock owner. Even a novice at options can implement the strategy properly by following the basic guidelines contained here. This is not to say that covered writing is necessarily the best strategy of all strategies that are available. But it may prove far superior to mere stock ownership, to which most investors will compare it.

It is certainly worth the time and effort of all stock owners to understand this strategy, whether or not they decide to use it as one of their own investment techniques. To that end, the clear, concise information presented in this text will provide that understanding so that educated stock owners can make the decision as to whether or not the strategy fits their personality and their investment needs.

—Lawrence G. McMillan

Introduction

To be clear up front, this is not another book about how to trade options. It is also not about exotic or highly speculative option strategies or about options on futures, bonds, or indexes. It is devoted to a single underutilized equity investing technique known as *covered call option writing*, which combines listed stocks with call options. Although any individual can employ the strategy, few actively practice it, and brokers generally will not tell you about it. Below you will learn why. The chapters to come will provide all the knowledge and tools necessary to implement this disciplined yet highly flexible investment technique.

Industry surveys consistently show that investors know little about options and view the instruments as too risky to suit their objectives. This opinion extends even to covered call writing, which is actually a conservative, risk-reducing strategy. It has, however, been tainted in the public eye by its association with other option strategies that are unquestionably at the high end of the risk spectrum.

The securities industry is not eager to remedy this situation. Today, while you can buy or write options through most securities firms, few encourage the practice. This has much to do with the industry's historical experience with these instruments. Options trading was formalized on exchanges like the Chicago Board Options Exchange and the American Stock Exchange in 1973. By 1981, according to the Options Clearing Corporation, annual volume in equity options exceeded 100 million contracts in a single year, and options on stocks had begun to generate considerable commissions for securities firms. But with these commissions came a surge in customer complaints, lawsuits, training expenses, and costly trading errors. Most firms concluded it made better business sense to avoid these liabilities by discouraging their retail clients from using the product altogether.

Another reason behind the industry's reticence on the subject of options is the burdensome nature of educating investors. Securities laws are severely restrictive about what brokers can provide as advice and education to their clients. And the firms' own in-house attorneys and compliance officers have been loath to allow them to offer any content in writing to the public that could in any way be used against them later if a client loses money. In addition, full service firms see educating clients as undermining their business model, which depends on the need for a broker's advice in order to justify their commission structures. Since 1975, moreover, knowledgeable investors have been flocking to discount brokers, with their streamlined, lower-fee business model. Thus, for a full-service firm, educating clients only increases the risk of losing them. Discount brokers, meanwhile, must rely on a clientele that is already investment-savvy, since their low cost structure makes education too expensive.

Then there is the difficulty of training and managing individual brokerage representatives with regard to options. Options activities are monitored more closely than stock activities by regulatory edict. That presents a daunting challenge for firms with hundreds or thousands of individual brokers. In addition, over the past twenty years, the big full-service brokerages have realized that they cannot compete against discounters for transaction-oriented clients and that handling this clientele keeps reps glued to their terminals all day, rather than out calling on new potential clients. As a result, they have been moving away from trading individual securities in favor of overall asset management. To this end, many firms have lowered the brokers' share of trading commissions. Thus, individual reps may be strongly discouraged from doing option business by their employers.

This book aims to counteract the pervasive prejudice against options and, by extension, covered writing. While other notable authors have touched on the virtues of the strategy, they have left out important aspects of the discussion and valuable insights. We attempt to fill the gaps by addressing topics such as the intangible benefits of covered writing (Chapter 6); its implementation as an ongoing strategy rather than as a single position (Chapters 4 and 7); the long-term results of covered option writing, explored through real data histories on individual stocks (Chapter 5); and the electronic tools now available for implementing covered writing (Chapter 9).

Another goal of *New Insights on Covered Call Writing* is to change your view of investing. One of the classic debates, for example, is about whether option trading is actually gambling. Aren't option buyers simply making a bet on the movement of the underlying stock? Certainly there are option buyers who use options in this manner. But the thousands of professional investment organizations—including pension funds, university endowments, and investment firms—that use options are not doing so because they are tired of flying to Las Vegas. They are taking advantage of a bona fide investment tool designed to enhance the overall returns of their stock portfolios.

If you are going to become a covered call writer, you must come to grips with the notion that you will have ongoing but brief affairs with stocks, and never marry one. Your investment planning will revolve around monthly option expirations rather than leaving stock as part of your estate. If that makes you a speculator in your own eyes, then you will have difficulty adopting this strategy. People who feel they must hold stocks for months, or even years, and then try to write calls against these stocks will inevitably run into problems. It is fine to invest in stocks for the long term, and it's fine to implement covered call writing—as long as you keep the two strategies separate in your mind as opposed to trying to combine them.

Beyond changing your investment perspective, the book aims to do the following:

- **Teach you everything you need to know to engage in covered call option writing as a self-managed investment technique.** You do not require any prior knowledge about options, but you should have minimal knowledge of and experience with stocks.
- **Present an objective view of the strategy.** We aim to point out in detail the benefits (both financial and emotional) as well as the risks.
- **Arm you with all the knowledge you need to tailor the strategy to your personal investment style regardless of**

how conservative or aggressive. Call writing can be implemented at a wide spectrum of risk levels. The book will guide you through the various ways to reduce or increase the strategy's risk (and thus its reward).

■ **Help you to develop realistic expectations.** As with just about any type of investing, you can succeed or fail in covered call writing independently of whether you made or lost money and how much. A growth-oriented money manager who achieves a 15 percent return when the broader market is up 12 percent may be quite happy with his results. He might also be happy with -5 percent if the market return is -20 percent. Either of those returns in a market that is up 25 percent for the period may be quite disappointing. A very conservative money manager might be pleased with all these performances, and a hedge fund manager happy with none. It is all about aligning your results to your objectives rather than looking at them in absolute terms.

Covered writing can represent a uniquely attractive investment strategy, but you will need to spend time learning the ropes. For some folks, options can be difficult to grasp and would therefore not be appropriate. You do not need a doctorate in mathematics to master the concept of covered writing, but you do need to understand the characteristics of a time-decaying financial asset and be familiar with the rules and terminology involved.

New Insights on Covered Call Writing: The Powerful Technique That Enhances Return and Lowers Risk in Stock Investing was written so that individual investors, brokers, or professional money managers can use the book to understand and fully implement a covered call writing program. Readers interested in continuing their options education might want to refer to coauthor Lawrence G. McMillan's other books, *Options as a Strategic Investment* and *McMillan on Options*, both of which are listed in the bibliography. In addition, you will find a great deal of information on options and on covered writing at the two authors' websites: **www.coveredwriter.com** and **www.optionstrategist.com**.

BUILDING THE FOUNDATION

TO UNDERSTAND AND IMPLEMENT COVERED CALL WRITING EFFEC-tively, you need to understand not only how stocks and the equity markets work, but what options are, how they function, and what affects their value. The book assumes you are already familiar with stocks. Part One provides a comprehensive review of equity options and the building blocks of a covered call writing strategy. If you are already familiar with options, you can begin with Part Two and refer back to Chapters 1, 2, and 3 as necessary. Recaps are included at the ends of Chapters 1 and 2 that also can serve as refreshers.

Option Basics 1

Everyone has the brainpower to follow the stock market. If you made it through fifth-grade math, you can do it.

PETER LYNCH, celebrated former manager of the Fidelity Magellan Fund

MOST INVESTMENT PROFESSIONALS WILL TELL YOU THAT THERE is no free lunch in investment management. Higher potential returns will always entail higher risk of one sort or another. Nevertheless, tens of thousands of money managers, portfolio managers, and other asset management professionals continually attempt to squeeze out better long-term risk-adjusted returns through an almost limitless variety of customized approaches to stock selection, asset allocation, technical analysis, hedging, and so on. For them, the Holy Grail is a strategy that generates measurably higher risk-adjusted performance than their competitors (or the market averages) can achieve. Some professionals and individuals believe they have found their Holy Grail in covered call writing.

Covered call writing consists of selling call options on stock whose shares you hold. Practiced for nearly thirty years by a small but dedicated number of investors, the strategy is arousing heightened interest in the institutional investment community as a result of analysis published by the Chicago Board Options Exchange in the spring of 2002. In May of that year, the CBOE created a new benchmark called the BuyWrite Index (BXM), which emulates an ongoing covered call writing strategy on the Standard & Poor's 500 Index. Extending the BXM back in time showed that the average annualized return hypothetically generated between 1988 and 2001 by a basic covered writing program would have been less than half a percentage point below that produced by owning the S&P 500 basket of stocks, but with markedly lower volatility in monthly returns. (The results of the study are discussed in detail in Chapter 5.) Holy Grail? Maybe not, but it certainly merits a look.

WHAT ARE OPTIONS?

Options are extraordinarily flexible instruments that can be used, either by themselves or in combination with other securities, in investment strategies running the gamut from highly speculative to ultraconservative. The price of this flexibility is complexity. This book will attempt to clarify the basics of stock options, including the rules and procedures for executing orders, how expirations and assignments work, tax treatment, and so on. More information is available on the Internet, from the Options Clearing Corporation (OCC), and the option exchanges (see the table at the end of Chapter 9 for the addresses of their websites).

An *option* is a contract representing the right, for a specified term, to buy or sell a specified security at a specified price. There are two types of options: *puts* and *calls*.

- **Call option:** A contract representing the right for a specified term to *buy* a specified security at a specified price.
- **Put option:** A contract representing the right for a specified time to *sell* a specified security at a specified price.

The specified price is known as the *strike*, or *exercise*, *price;* the specified term is determined by the option's *expiration date;* and the specified security is referred to as the *underlying security*. There are exchange-listed options on a number of securities, including indexes and bonds, but this book is devoted entirely to those on stocks, otherwise known as *equity options.* A standard equity option represents 100 shares of the underlying stock. Thus a call option on Disney with a strike price of $25 that expires in two months gives the buyer the right, during the next two months, to buy 100 shares of Disney at $25 each.

- **Strike price:** The price at which the underlying security of an option can be purchased or sold by the contract buyer.
- **Expiration:** The date when the terms of an option contract terminate.
- **Underlying security:** The security that an option gives its buyer the right to buy or sell.

How Options Compare with Stock

Options have a number of important distinctions from stocks, but it is helpful to begin with the similarities. Companies issue stock in compliance with a host of securities laws that govern their activities on behalf of the public. When you buy shares of stock through an initial public offering (IPO), you pay money to the company in return for certain rights, such as the rights to vote, to receive any dividends the company pays out, and to realize any increases in shareholder equity that occur. These rights are what give your stock value. They are guaranteed by a stock certificate, which you may never actually see—your broker keeps it for safekeeping unless you request it.

The initial arrangement is between you and the issuing company. Once the stock is available on the secondary market (through formal exchanges), shares can be purchased from, or sold to, someone else, since they are standardized—that is, shares held by one individual are identical to those held by another (as long as they are of the same type or class, such as common or preferred).

An option is also an agreement between you and another party, but in this case the other party could be almost anyone: a company, a professional trader, a market maker, or another individual investor. As with stock, the buyers of options pay money in return for certain rights, acknowledged by the selling parties. The role of option sellers is similar to that of the issuing company in the stock scenario, in that they receive money and are thus obligated to fulfill the specified rights conferred on the buyers. Options have value because of what these rights represent. They too are standardized, so they can trade on formal securities exchanges, and are regulated by the Securities and Exchange Commission (SEC).

Now for some differences. Options are classified as *derivatives* because their value is *derived* from the underlying security. Option holders do not have the right to vote or to receive regular dividends, as stockholders do. They are, however, affected by stock splits, spin-offs, and other significant corporate events.

When corporations issue stock, they offer a fixed number of shares to the public. That number remains fixed until the company either issues more shares, splits them, or buys some back. An option contract, in contrast, is not issued until a buyer and seller come together in the marketplace. When an exchange initiates trading on a particular option, no contract exists until the first transaction takes place. The option is issued when party A agrees to buy one from party B, and additional contracts are issued as other buyers and sellers make deals.

Standardization

Although options contracts are legally binding, you need not call your attorney to draw one up when you want either to buy or to sell. Option contracts are originated and standardized by an independent entity called the Options Clearing Corporation (OCC). To comply with SEC regulations, the OCC files a prospectus for all options on behalf of all the buyers and sellers. It also sets, guarantees, and enforces all contract terms and keeps the master versions of all contracts. You see only a trade confirmation, as you most often do with stocks. (If you are curious, you can see the OCC prospectus on the Internet at www.optionsclearing.com under Publications.)

■ **OCC:** The Options Clearing Corp., an independent entity that acts as the issuer and guarantor for all listed option contracts.

By standardizing contracts, the OCC enables options to be traded in the secondary market (on an exchange), just like a listed stock or bond. In other words, they are *interchangeable*, or *fungible*. When you buy 100 shares of Disney common stock for your account, you know that those shares are exactly the same as any other Disney common shares. Similarly, the OCC guarantees that when you buy a particular Disney call option, your contract has the same terms— that is, it is for the same type of option, on the same underlying stock, with the same strike price and expiration—as all others referred to with the same designation. All options having identical terms are said to be part of the same series and are interchangeable.

- ▪ **Class:** All the options of the same type that have the same underlying security. For example, all the call options that exist for Microsoft stock are part of the same option class .
- ▪ **Series:** All the options in the same class that also have the same strike price and expiration date. For example, all IBM calls in January with a strike price of 90 are part of the same option series.

Listed versus Unlisted

Listed options are those that are formally traded on a recognized exchange. *Non-listed*, or *over-the-counter*, options also exist, but they are used infrequently and only by institutions. Individual investors need be concerned only with listed options. All the options reported in the newspapers or through quote services are listed. Occasionally an option may be listed on more than one exchange. This does not affect the option's interchangeability. Option exchanges generally trade during the same hours as the underlying stocks plus a few extra minutes at the end of the day (4:02 P.M. Eastern time), except on the Friday before expiration, when they stop trading right at 4 P.M.

The OCC plays another important role: as intermediary between option buyers and sellers. When you buy or sell an option, you are actually dealing directly with the OCC (through your broker), rather than with a particular individual. That means you do not need to worry about the integrity of the transaction or about the other party's ability to pay. His or her broker worries about that.

OPTION LISTINGS

The option exchanges determine what options they will list—in other words, which underlying stocks they will allow options to trade on. Thus IBM, for instance, has no say as to whether options are listed on its shares or not. Currently, options are available on approximately 2,300 stocks, with new listings added every month. The reason that figure is so small compared with the total universe of listed stocks is that only certain stocks meet the exchanges' requirements. Because of the close relationship between options and their underlying securities, primary among the exchanges' criteria are that the underlying stocks be listed and actively traded on a national market. Other requirements concern the number of shares outstanding, the stock's price history, its daily trading volume, the company's assets, and so on. As an example, new options listings are not approved for stocks trading below $7.50.

Since 100 shares is the standard contract size for a single option, you only need to identify any option by the four items that make it unique: underlying stock; expiration month; strike price; and type. The table below, for example, shows that IBM Jan 85 call designates a call option on IBM shares, expiring in January, with a strike price of 85.

Examples:

Underlying Security	Expiration Month	Strike Price	Type
Disney	Oct	25	Put
Home Depot	Aug	50	Call
IBM	Jan	85	Call
Intel	Apr	25	Call
Microsoft	Jul	50	Put

Strike Price

Options on a particular stock are almost always available for at least several different strike prices, the number depending on the stock's price and volatility (how much the share price has moved in a given period). A volatile stock such as IBM, for example, could have options with as many as fifteen strike prices at any one time. It is not necessary or practical to have options available for every price at which a stock has ever traded. The option exchanges offer strikes in increments of $2.50, $5, or $10, depending on the price of the underlying stock. Thus, if XYZ is selling for around $50 a share when options trading on the stock begins, the exchange would typically allow trading (for both puts and calls) on a range of strike prices including, say, $40, $45, $50, $55, and $60. On the other hand, if the share price is $16, you would probably see strike prices of $15, $17.50, and $20. As stocks move, new strike prices are added, although the exchanges generally do not add new strikes during the last few weeks before an expiration.

Depending on the price of the underlying stock at the time, options at various strike prices are said to be *in the money* or *out of the money*. These terms are important to the covered writer and will be referred to frequently in the text.

- **In the money:** Describes a *call* option whose strike price is *below* the current price of the underlying stock or a *put* with a strike *above* the current price. *Example:* When ABC stock is trading at $43, call options with strike prices of 40, 35, and 30 are all in the money.
- **Out of the money:** Describes a *call* option whose strike price is *above* the current price of the underlying stock or a *put* with a strike *below* the current price. *Example:* When ABC stock is trading at $43, call options with strike prices of 45, 50, and 55 are all out of the money.
- **At the money:** Describes an option that has a strike price equal to (or close to) the current price of the underlying stock. *Example:* A GHI call option with a strike of 30 is at the money when the stock is trading at or very close to $30.

Expiration

Options' most distinctive characteristic is their limited life, determined by their expiration date. On that date, they, and any value they may have contained, cease to exist. In contrast, when bonds "mature," they can no longer be traded but they do make their last interest payment and repay their principal. Options' short life—never longer than nine months for standard contracts—is one of the properties making covered call writing a viable strategy.

To keep things standardized, all the options expiring in a particular month do so on the same day: the Saturday following that month's third Friday. Sounds weird, but they made it Saturday to give brokers one last morning following the last trading day to reconcile their clients' positions and make sure there are no errors going into expiration. The third Friday of each month is therefore the last day expiring options can be traded. Expiring options can be bought or sold as usual on this Friday, but trading is frequently heavier than average, as people close out positions before they expire.

PLAYERS AND POSITIONS

The buyers of an option are considered *holders*. This is a virtual term only; there is nothing physical to hold. In fact, there are no certificates with options—everything is done by book entry. But since the buyers pay money, they are considered owners of the options. As with stock, when you buy an option you create a *long* position in your account.

The option seller is also called the *writer*. Again, this is just a label, a holdover from the old days, when put and call contracts were actually written by people who owned stock and offered these options for sale. Writers receive money, and their position is considered *short*. The terms *buying* and *selling* are actions. The terms *long* and *short* describe positions, indicating whether you actually have possession of the asset or not.

As with stocks, you can initiate an option position by buying (going long) or selling (selling short) as your *opening transaction*. With covered writing, your opening transaction is to sell one or more call options short. Once you have become either a holder or a writer of an option, you can close your position anytime before expiration, as long as the option is trading, simply by executing an *offsetting*, or *closing*, transaction at the prevailing market price. The only catch is that you must accept the market price for the option in effect at the time. To close a short position in a call option on XYZ stock, for example, you would simply buy a call on XYZ with the same strike and expiration. When you close your option position, you wipe the slate clean, completely eliminating any further rights or obligations from prior contracts.

Since you can initiate an option position by either buying or selling, four scenarios are possible when you enter any option order. You may

- buy to open (if you are simply buying a put or call)
- buy to close (if you are already short an option and are closing out)
- sell to open (if you are initiating a covered write)
- sell to close (if you had previously bought an option and are now closing)

It is standard practice throughout the industry to require you to indicate on every option order whether you are opening or closing. (You will also usually be asked whether an opening sale is *covered* or *naked*; for a discussion of these terms, see below.) This information does not affect your trade or the price in any way.

- **Holders:** Those who initiate a position by buying an option. They do not actually hold anything physical. What they hold is the right to buy or sell stock.
- **Writers:** Those who initiate a position by selling an option. Writers are obligated to fulfill the buyers' right to buy or sell stock. They do not actually write anything, though in the very early days of option contracts, it would generally have been the seller who would have written a contract and offered it for sale.
- **Long:** Term used to describe the position of an option holder.
- **Short:** Term used to describe the position of an option writer.

EXERCISE AND ASSIGNMENT

The Basic Mechanics

When holders wish to invoke the right, given them by their option, to buy or sell the underlying stock, they are said to exercise their option. This is accomplished by informing their broker. Notice can be verbal, just like placing an order to buy or sell stock (which is essentially what an exercise is anyway). Thus, if you hold a call option for DEF stock and you decide to exercise, you are essentially entering a buy order for DEF at the strike price, except that your order would be routed to the OCC rather than directly to the exchange where the stock trades. Exercises take effect at night after the close of trading. Since the price is determined by the option strike, it does not matter what time of day an option is exercised.

Options that can be exercised at any time before expiration are said to be *American style;* those that can be exercised only at expiration are called *European style* or *capped.* This has nothing to do with where they trade. Equity options on individual stocks all trade American style. Index options trade European style.

As noted above, the standard *contract size* (or *unit of trading*) is 100 shares. That is the number of shares that the writer must deliver if a holder exercises the contract. These shares are sometimes referred to as the *deliverable.* There are listed options on common stocks as well as on some preferred stocks and ADRs (American Depositary Receipts on foreign securities) and on various other financial instruments, including futures and stock indexes. Index options may stipulate *cash delivery* instead of *physical delivery,* because of the practical considerations of buying every stock in an index. All equity options require physical delivery of the underlying shares. The process of actually delivering an underlying security as part of an option exercise is called *settlement* and is handled by your broker just like the settlement of a regular stock transaction.

When an option is exercised by one or more holders, the OCC must determine who in the writers pool to *assign* that exercise to for fulfillment—in other words, which writer has to sell his or her stock. The notification process is referred to as an *assignment.* The OCC keeps the master record of which accounts at which member brokerage firms are either short or long every option. It distributes assignments by passing them to member firms that have open short positions and letting *them* figure out which of their customer accounts get assigned. The brokerage firms must have fair and reasonable ways to distribute assignments, but they do not all have to be the same. Some firms select randomly, while others use a first in/first out policy.

Receiving an assignment notice from your broker is essentially the same as receiving a trade confirmation for selling shares of stock, except that you did not have to enter an order—it was generated by the assignment notice. This should occur early in the morning following the exercise, but there is no guarantee on the exact time. The broker gets word during the night and will want to let you know right away so that you do not unknowingly close your call position or sell your stock in the market that day. (Writers are not allowed to close a position once they have been assigned, even if the broker has not yet informed them of the assignment.) As soon as any of your short options are assigned, that, of course, eliminates those positions.

Say a holder of 5 Philip Morris June 50 calls decides to exercise them. The OCC informs Charles Schwab that it is being handed an assignment for the calls. You are among the clients at Schwab who are short the Philip Morris June 50 calls. You happen to have 1,000 shares of the stock and are short 10 calls. Schwab informs you that "you have been assigned on 5 MO Jun 50 calls," and you subsequently receive a trade confirmation that you sold 500 shares of MO at $50. You are left with 500 shares and 5 short calls—plus $25,000, less commission, added to your account.

- ■ **Exercise:** The action that option holders take when they notify their brokers of their intent to invoke the right to buy (or sell) stock as stipulated in their option. When call holders exercise, they are purchasing the underlying stock at the designated strike price.
- ■ **Settlement:** The process of delivering an underlying security (or other stipulated interest) as a result of an option exercise. Stock options always stipulate physical delivery of the underlying shares.
- ■ **Assignment:** The action that the OCC and your broker take in selecting option sellers (writers) to fulfill the obligation stipulated by the option they sold. When call writers receive assignment notices from their brokers, they are selling the underlying stock at the designated strike price.

Since the OCC is the intermediary for all option transactions and assignments, it is able to keep track of how many contracts are outstanding at all times and determines at the end of each day how many are "open" (remain unclosed). The OCC publishes this number each day as the *open interest.*

▪ **Open interest:** The number of existing contracts that remain unclosed for a particular option. This figure is usually published each trading day by the OCC and is net of all trades that have occurred up to the close of the previous day. In conjunction with the daily volume of contracts traded, it provides an indication of the option's liquidity (how easily it can be traded).

What Happens at Expiration

Expiration is the grand finale of the option opera. Once trading stops at the end of the Friday before an expiration Saturday, the only other actions that can take place are exercise and assignment. By Monday morning, that option is history. You won't even see it among your account holdings anymore, although you will generally see the expiration on your activity screen. If you were short a particular option, however, you will receive notification from your broker confirming whether it expired or was assigned.

By the time expiring options stop trading on Friday afternoon, the ones that are in the money will generally be in the hands of market makers and other professionals who will exercise them. Most speculators will have traded out and closed their positions. Regardless of who owns the options, however, you can expect them to be exercised. If they are in the money by more than $0.75, they will be exercised automatically (by OCC rules), but even if they are only in the money by a nickel or a dime, they will usually be exercised. Otherwise someone would be throwing away money, and don't count on that happening too often. If the stock and strike prices are really close (or identical), you may or may not be assigned. If you ever have a question about whether you were assigned following an expiration where the stock is close to your strike price, check your account on

Monday morning to be sure, and don't feel bashful about asking your broker to be certain.

Something many call holders may not realize is that your brokerage firm can exercise your call options for its own account if you do not exercise them for yours. If you have a call that is in the money by, say, $0.25 and you decide that the commissions would eat up this cash value, you might just let it expire without exercising. Your brokerage firm can then exercise your calls and sell the stock on Monday morning. Since brokers do not pay commissions, the economics might work out for them. If your brokerage firm takes such action, it does not affect you at all, and you will receive no communication of their action.

By the way, you *do* pay commissions on exercises and assignments, since they are essentially the equivalent of buy and sell orders.

COVERED VERSUS NAKED

When you write a call option, you are contractually obligated to deliver (sell) the underlying stock if assigned. If you own enough of the underlying stock to make good on this obligation, then your option is considered *covered*. It's like saying it is *secured* in the banking world. Since you own the underlying stock, writing a covered call option entails no additional risk: You can deliver the stock upon being assigned, regardless of the share price at the time. If, on the other hand, the stock is not in your account when you write the call, your option position is considered uncovered, or *naked*. An uncovered call option exposes you to a theoretically unlimited loss if the stock goes way up, because you will have to buy it to fulfill your obligation to the OCC and the option holder when the contract is exercised.

The fact that one option contract represents 100 shares of stock means that you must remember this *multiplier* (100) when figuring how many contracts to buy or sell. To sell (write) options on more than 100 shares, you would simply sell multiple option contracts. For 300 shares, you could sell up to three contracts. For 1,000 shares, you could sell up to 10 contracts, and so on. There is no way to sell an option for fewer than 100 shares. So if you happen to have an odd number of shares, such as 458, you will only be able to write covered calls against 400 shares.

Very important: When entering orders, if you own 500 shares of a stock and you want to write calls, you must remember to enter an order for 5 calls, not 500! Your broker or your online service would probably catch your mistake, but you should make a note to avoid that kind of error.

You can certainly have *more* than the required amount of shares in your account than you need to deliver if your calls are assigned. Say you own 1,000 shares of DEF and sell 6 DEF calls. You would at most have to deliver 600 shares if assigned, so you're completely covered. But if you have 1,000 shares and sell 12 calls, then 2 of those calls are naked.

Examples:

Stock Position	Option Position	Status
Long 500 ABC	Short 5 ABC calls	Fully covered
Long 600 DEF	Short 4 DEF calls	Fully covered
Long 800 GHI	Short 10 GHI calls	8 calls covered; 2 calls naked
Long 0 JKL	Short 4 JKL calls	4 calls naked

- ▪ **Covered:** Describes a short option position that is secured by a long position in the underlying stock sufficient to fulfill an assignment.
- ▪ **Naked (uncovered):** Describes a short option position that is not secured by shares of the underlying stock.

OPTIONS IN YOUR ACCOUNT

Industry regulations require that brokerage firms preapprove all customers who wish to buy or sell options. There are no exceptions to this process, and you cannot buy or sell a single option until you are approved. Even if you are just going to write covered calls, which does not entail nearly the same risk as buying options or selling naked options, you will still have to be approved by your firm. It will require you to fill out and sign an Option Agreement, separate from your new account form, and provide you with a copy of the booklet *Characteristics and Risks of Standardized Options,* also referred to as the options disclosure document. You can trade options in multiple accounts, but you must be approved in each account. If you have a joint account with someone else, that person will also need to sign the Option Agreement.

When you fill out an Option Agreement, you are required to indicate which strategies you intend to use, and you will be approved for specific strategies only. Some firms combine the various strategies into two or three general risk categories and approve you for one of them. Covered call writing will always be in the lowest risk category. However, it may be lumped together with a strategy like option buying, which carries much more risk but still not as much as strategies such as writing naked calls.

To initiate a naked option position, you must not only acquire preapproval but also secure the position with a hefty amount of cash or margin. If you are approved for covered writing but not naked writing, then you must always have or purchase the stock before selling calls against it. If you want to sell the call first and try to buy the stock at a lower price sometime later, your broker will not let you unless you are approved to sell naked options (and it's not a wise practice anyway).

RECAPPING OPTION BASICS

- An *option* is an exchange-listed financial instrument regulated by the SEC. It is a *contract* between two parties.

- There are two *types* of options: A *call* option represents the right to *buy* a specified security. A *put* option represents the right to *sell* a specified security.

- Option contracts are issued and guaranteed by the *Options Clearing Corp. (OCC).* The OCC sets and enforces all contract terms, ensuring that all option contracts are standardized and interchangeable. The OCC also acts as the intermediary between all option buyers and sellers.

- All options trade by book entry; there are no certificates.

■ The buyer is the *holder* and is *long* the option. The seller is the *writer* and is *short* the option. The buyer has certain rights that the seller is obligated to fulfill.

■ An *equity option* represents *100 shares* of a specified stock. It is important to remember the multiplier (100) when figuring how many contracts to buy or sell.

■ If the option is *exercised,* the writer must *deliver* shares of the underlying stock.

■ The *strike price* of the option is the price at which the holder may buy (or sell) the underlying security. If the stock is trading above the strike price of a call option, the call is said to be *in the money.* If the stock is trading below the strike price of a call option, then the call is considered *out of the money.* If the stock is trading very close to the strike price of a call option, the call is said to be *at the money.*

■ Options *expire* on a specified date. Expirations for different options occur in all calendar months and are standardized to occur on the Saturday following the third Friday of the stipulated month.

■ Options on stocks can be *exercised* at any time before expiration. When a holder exercises, a writer must be *assigned.* When a call option is exercised, the OCC *assigns* a writer of those options to fulfill the obligation of the contract—that is, sell the underlying stock at the strike price. The OCC does this by assigning a member broker who in turn assigns one or more clients.

Just Beyond the Basics   2

Investors operate with limited funds and limited intelligence; they don't need to know everything. As long as they understand something better than others, they have an edge.

GEORGE SOROS, famed financier and financial philosopher

OPTION BUYERS AND SELLERS HAVE A COMMON INTEREST: THE option's *price*, also called its *premium*. The price is determined by the marketplace and is quoted on a per share basis. Since each contract represents 100 shares, the amount of money you actually pay for or receive from an option is 100 times the quoted price. Thus, if a call is quoted at 2.25, the contract will have a total premium of $225 (on which brokerage commissions are figured).

VALUING OPTIONS

The price or premium of an option has two components: *intrinsic*, or *cash*, *value* and *extrinsic*, or *time*, *value*. Intrinsic value is defined as the amount, if any, by which an option is in the money—in other words, how much money it is worth at this moment based on the current market price of the underlying shares. For a call option, this value is determined by how far above the option's strike price the stock is trading. Out-of-the-money options have zero intrinsic value. Any premium value over and above the cash value is the option's time value. The simple relationship between intrinsic and time value can be expressed as follows:

intrinsic value + time value = total value (premium)

As an illustration, consider the following situation:

Pfizer stock is selling at $42.50/share
Pfizer Jun 40 calls are 2.80
Pfizer Jun 45 calls are 0.55

The Pfizer Jun 40 call is in the money and has a current intrinsic (cash) value of $2.50. This stems from the fact that one could hypothetically pocket $2.50 per share by exercising the call (thereby purchasing stock at $40) and then selling the purchased shares for the market price of $42.50 each. The option's time value is $0.30, the amount by which the premium exceeds the intrinsic value. The Pfizer Jun 45 calls have a strike higher than the current share price, so they are out of the money. Their premium, $0.55, is thus entirely time value. An option could have a *negative* time value, although this is rare. Options do, however, frequently show time values of zero or almost zero as they get close to expiration.

- **Premium:** The price of an option or, more accurately, the money you pay or receive when you buy or sell it (per-share price times 100 shares).
- **Intrinsic, or cash, value:** The amount, if any, by which an option is in the money. Example: An ABC call option with a strike of 40 has $3 of intrinsic value if ABC is trading at $43. The same option has zero intrinsic value if ABC is trading anywhere below $40.
- **Time value:** The amount, if any, by which an option's premium exceeds its intrinsic value. Example: If ABC is trading at $43, an ABC call option with a strike of 40 that is trading at 5 has $2 of time value. The same option has zero time value if it is trading at 3.

▪ **Parity:** An in-the-money option that trades exactly at its intrinsic value is said to trade at parity.

Fair, or Theoretical, Value

Although options' actual prices, like those of stocks, are determined by the fluctuating dynamics of supply and demand, participants in both markets calculate where they believe a particular security *should* be trading. The relationship of this *fair,* or *theoretical, value* to the security's actual price—above, below, or equal—will help them decide whether to buy, sell, or hold it. Ask ten knowledgeable research analysts for the fair value of a stock they follow, however, and you are likely to get ten very different answers. That's because myriad factors can be used to determine the answer, and there is no agreement on which to use or how to evaluate them. Valuing options involves far fewer factors. There is, moreover, a widely accepted formula for combining them to calculate a theoretical value for any listed option. This is the Black-Scholes formula, named after the two University of Chicago professors, Fisher Black and Myron Scholes, who first proposed it in 1973. This formula, for which Myron Scholes later earned the Nobel Prize for Economics, has become the accepted standard for valuing options throughout the industry.

The factors incorporated into the Black-Scholes formula are:

▪ Price of the underlying stock
▪ Strike price of the option
▪ Amount of time left until expiration
▪ Volatility of the underlying stock
▪ Interest rates
▪ Dividends on the underlying stock

Volatility

Although everyone uses the same Black-Scholes formula, you may see different theoretical prices on the same option from different sources. The variable in the formula that accounts for these differences is *volatility.*

Volatility is a measure of how much a security has moved (or potentially *can* move) in a given amount of time either up or down. It is extremely important in determining an option's theoretical value, because it is the factor in the formula that essentially accounts for the *probability* that the underlying stock can move to or beyond the strike price before the expiration date. If a high-flying semiconductor stock and a conservative bank stock are both trading at $30 a share, would you say that both have the same probability of reaching $35 by a certain date? No. Their historical trading ranges would very likely be quite different, resulting in different historical volatilities. This difference in volatility has a substantial impact on the price of their options.

Volatility is calculated using the statistical formula for the standard deviation of a set of historical values. The rub is that different people use differently defined sets. Some use short periods, such as 20 or 50 days, while others use 100 days or even one year. Each of these time periods can yield a different volatility value. The greater rub is that *none* of the historical probability periods may produce an accurate prediction of the stock's future volatility. It is important to know all this so that you can keep a realistic perspective on the theoretical prices you see for options on quote screens or other services. (More detailed discussions of volatility and how premiums vary with strike price, volatility, and time can be found in Chapters 5 and 8.)

Interest Rates

The inclusion of interest rates in the formula may surprise you. They do play a role in determining option prices, although a very minor one. In fact, the impact of interest rates will be imperceptible unless they change dramatically in a short period of time. Even if they do, the effect on covered writing is nothing like that on fixed-yield investments. The role interest rates play in option pricing stems from the cost an arbitrageur would have to pay to carry a *riskless* stock-and-option position. (For a discussion of option arbitrage and its effect on option prices, see Chapter 8.) Option writers can expect to get very slightly higher option premiums when interest rates are higher, all other things being equal.

Dividends

Option prices are affected by dividends, although some models omit them for convenience. A dividend is a cash distribution to shareholders from the earnings of the company. Once paid, it is no longer part of the company's net worth. To reflect this fact, the stock price is reduced on the appropriate date by the amount of the dividend (and thus trades "ex-dividend" on that date). One would expect call options to be priced somewhat lower for stocks paying dividends, since the option buyer gets no benefit from the payout. Furthermore, the dividend represents value that is *removed* from the company's net worth each quarter rather than being reinvested inside the company and thus reduces the growth prospects of the stock. The value of a call option does tend to be lower on a dividend stock because buyers know the stock price will be lowered on the ex-dividend date. Since the value of the call option depends on the price of the stock, the call option will tend to anticipate this drop as the dividend approaches.

High-dividend stocks, therefore, tend to have call options with smaller premiums. If you do write calls on a dividend-paying stock and they are in the money when the dividend record date nears, you also need to be alert to the possibility of an early exercise by a call holder who wants the stock before the dividend is paid.

Theory versus Reality

Just about everyone in the options world uses the Black-Scholes formula to determine the theoretical price of an option. The key word here is *theoretical.* The actual price in the market is whatever a buyer and seller agree to, and this agreement is shaped by considerations beyond those incorporated in the formula. *Characteristics and Risks of Standardized Options,* the booklet the options exchanges give to those opening option accounts, lists the factors that can affect the actual price of an option. Among those not included in the Black-Scholes model are:

- The current values of related interests (other stocks, index futures, and so on)
- The style of the option (American, European)
- The depth of the market for that option (liquidity)
- Supply and demand in the options market
- Supply and demand in the market for the underlying equity
- Estimates or expectations for future developments

As a result of considerations like these, actual market prices for options can be quite different from their theoretical values. But the formula provides an important benchmark that determines whether an option is (at least theoretically) overvalued or undervalued. The pros rely quite heavily on Black-Scholes, and it helps determine where the specialists and market makers at the exchanges set their bids and offers. Many option price screens will provide the Black-Scholes theoretical value as a reference when quoting the actual price and volume. More often than not, options trade at prices higher than their theoretical values, which is good news for covered writers.

Although an option's market price can fluctuate during the trading day, various market factors tend to keep it aligned with the price of the underlying stock. (Primary among these is arbitrage, which will be discussed in Chapter 8.) If the underlying stock rises, for instance, the prices of call options on it will generally move up as well, by different amounts depending on each contract's strike price. Intraday fluctuations are of critical interest to traders, though they will also affect strategies like covered writing, albeit to a lesser degree.

The bottom line for a basic covered call writer is this: When you are looking for attractive investment opportunities, your focus should be on identifying a stock that meets your criteria and a call option that offers an attractive return. Whether the option is higher or lower than its theoretical value because of market factors might be critical to a trader and useful to an advanced covered writer, but it should be of only minor concern to the basic covered writer. It will be beneficial to understand why an option is priced where it is, but it is not critical to the effective implementation of the covered writing strategy.

TRADING SYMBOLS

Finding options prices in the newspaper these days is challenging. There are simply too many available to print them all. Most general newspapers have stopped printing option prices at all, preferring instead to print the closing prices and net asset values (NAVs) of mutual funds, because more people own these investments. Even the *Wall Street Journal* carries only an abbreviated listing of the most active options. This is not altogether bad news, since there is now far more option data available on the Internet than there ever was in the newspapers.

In newspapers, options are usually listed alphabetically by the name of the underlying stock, but in the online world, you can get a direct quote with an option symbol, or you can look up all the available options on a particular stock with the stock symbol. Online option quotes are free at numerous sites on the Internet. (See Chapter 7 for details and the end of Chapter 9 for a list of Internet-based resources for covered writers.)

Option symbols are made up of three to five letters, depending on the stock symbol. They are created as follows:

stock symbol (or "root")	1–3 letters depending upon symbol
	+
option type and expiration	1 letter (see table)
	+
strike price	1 letter (see table)

For stock symbols consisting of four letters, the exchanges create a three-letter root to use instead. Cisco, for example, has the ticker CSCO on the Nasdaq. Since this is too long, the exchange designates the root CYQ for Cisco options.

The letters used to specify an option's terms for symbol purposes are as follows:

Type and Expiration

Calls		Puts	Calls		Puts
A	January	M	G	July	S
B	February	N	H	August	T
C	March	O	I	September	U
D	April	P	J	October	V
E	May	Q	K	November	W
F	June	R	L	December	X

Strike Prices

5 or 105	A	75 or 175		O
10 or 110	B	80 or 180		P
15 or 115	C	85 or 185		Q
20 or 120	D	90 or 195		R
25 or 125	E	95 or 195		S
30 or 130	F	100 or 200		T
35 or 135	G	**$2.50 Strikes**		
40 or 140	H	7.50		U
45 or 145	I	12.50		V
50 or 150	J	17.50		W
55 or 155	K	22.50		X
60 or 160	L	27.50		Y
65 or 165	M	32.50		Z
70 or 170	N			

Examples:

Abbott Apr 60 call	ABTDL
Cisco Jul 17.50 call	CYQGW
General Electric Jun 30 call	GEFF
JP Morgan Chase Jun 30 put	JPMRF

The exchanges frequently have to change option symbols as a result of adjustments being made to those contracts after they were issued. These adjustments are discussed next.

Adjustments

When certain events affecting an underlying security occur—such as a stock split, merger, or spin-off—the terms of the option contract need to be adjusted so that both holders and writers have essentially the same position after the event as they did before it. These adjustments may affect strike price and number of underlying shares, but never expiration date.

Say XYZ Corp. decides to split its stock two-for-one. The company is issuing an additional share for each one currently outstanding, and the share price is consequently cut in half. Stockholders thus retain the same percentage ownership in XYZ Corp. after the split as before. But the holder of an unadjusted call option on XYZ would have the right to buy 100 shares that represent only half as much ownership in the company as before. The terms of option need to change to reflect the change in the underlying stock.

Adjustments are decided upon, and effected by, a joint panel of the option exchanges and the OCC. In the XYZ example, on the effective date of the split, both holders and writers of existing options on the stock would have the number of their contracts doubled and the strike prices of these contracts halved. The before-and-after scenario is illustrated in the table below.

Stockholder

Before Stock Split	After Stock Split
XYZ is at $85/share	XYZ is at $42.50/share
Owner has 200 shares	Owner has 400 shares

Option Writer

Before Stock Split	After Stock Split
Writer is short	Writer is short
2 XYZ Jan 85 calls	4 Jan 42.5 calls

Odd splits, such as 3-for-2 or 5-for-4, can yield even stranger fractional strike prices, such as 16.7. For these odd splits, the number of shares represented by one contract may also change—to 133 or 150, say—to match the new strike price.

Regular cash dividends (those equal to less than 10 percent of the value of the stock) are not considered sufficient to adjust the terms of an option. The rationale is that these dividends are built into the price of the stock over time and do not materially change the value enough to warrant specific option adjustments. Besides, it would be impractical to do so every time a company issued a regular dividend.

When a company spins off a new entity, shares in the spin-off become part of the deliverable in outstanding option contracts. If company XYZ, for example, issues 10 shares of QRS for each 100 shares of XYZ common, a contract formerly calling for the delivery of 100 shares of XYZ will now call for 100 shares of XYZ and 10 shares of QRS.

As a covered writer, since you own the underlying stock, you will know when events such as a spin-off are going to occur. You can also check the CBOE website to look up information regarding an option adjustment. In cases where the number of shares on the contract is changed, the exchange also changes the option symbol so that it will be differentiated from the standard contract on 100 shares.

Adjustments will generally not represent a problem for an existing covered writing position. When initiating new positions, however, make sure that the option you write matches the shares you own; 100 shares of stock, for example, would not adequately cover a short option that was adjusted to 150 shares. And when closing a position that has been adjusted, check to see what the new symbol is.

Expiration Months

One glance at an option table in the *Wall Street Journal* or on a computer shows that options on different stocks have expirations in different months. It may look bizarre to have options on one stock expire in January, February, April, and July while options on the next one expire in January, February, May, and August. Actually, there is a logic to this, although it is a bit obscure. When options first began to trade on formal exchanges, in the 1970s, it was decided that for every stock, three-month, six-month, and nine-month options would initially be made available. Then, when the three months passed and the first option expired, a new nine-month option would be added on to the end. It was done that way because there was not enough volume (liquidity) in the beginning to justify having options expiring every month for individual stocks, and because the quarterly cycle enabled the exchanges to offer option expirations that corresponded to the quarterly earnings calendar of the underlying companies.

So, in the beginning, options were designated to expire in one of the following three quarterly cycles:

1 January-April-July-October
2 February-May-August-November
3 March-June-September-December

Only three of the cycle months would be available at any one time and when the nearest expiration passed, the next one in the calendar cycle would be added. If ABC options were introduced in cycle #1, they might begin trading with expirations in January, April, and July. On the Monday after the January options expired, the exchange would allow trading in October options, so that there would once again be three expiration months available.

For stocks on the January cycle, the process worked as follows (expiration months are highlighted):

As of January 1:	**JAN** Feb Mar **APR** May Jun **JUL**
When January options expired:	Feb Mar **APR** May Jun **JUL** Aug Sep **OCT**
When April options expired:	May Jun **JUL** Aug Sep **OCT** Nov Dec **JAN**

...and so on.

It became evident, however, that both option buyers and sellers were more interested in the *near-month* expirations (the current calendar month and the next one out) than in the ones three to nine months away. Reacting to this, the exchanges permitted the addition of two near-month expirations while keeping intact the quarterly cycle structure for the months farther out. So, today, instead of only three available expiration months at any one time, there are four—the two nearest months and the next two months in the quarterly cycle. The January cycle now works as follows:

As of January 1:   **JAN FEB** Mar **APR** May Jun **JUL**
(February is now added so that there will be two near-month expirations.)

When January options expire: **FEB MAR APR** May Jun **JUL**
(March is added as the second near month.)

When February options expire: **MAR APR** May Jun **JUL** Aug Sep **OCT**
(There are already two near months, so October is added as the next quarterly month.)

Don't feel that you need to memorize these rules. Just be aware that there will always be two near-month options available for each stock, and two expiration months farther out that will vary from stock to stock.

Since their inception in 1990, options with greater than nine-month terms have also been available. They are called *LEAPS* (long-term equity anticipation securities) and are available on about 300 stocks at the present time. LEAPS always expire in January and may be available as far out as three years. Otherwise, they work the same way as regular listed options. LEAPS are initially issued under different symbols to distinguish them from shorter-term options expiring in January, but as time brings them into the normal option expiration cycle, their symbols are changed and they become the regular January option. (LEAPS will be discussed further in Chapter 8.)

How Options Are Traded

The Exchanges

There are two types of trading systems employed by the stock and option exchanges: The *specialist system* and the *market-maker system*. In the specialist system, a single person (actually a single firm) facilitates the market. When there are no external buyers or sellers, the specialist is responsible for providing both a bid and an offer from his or her own account, at which the public can transact. In the market-maker system, several competing market makers perform the same function. Stocks on the NYSE and American Exchange trade under a specialist system, while those on the Nasdaq exchange trade through remotely located market makers who are connected electronically. Options on the Amex or Philadelphia exchanges trade by specialist, whereas the CBOE uses an exchange-based market-maker system. At the CBOE, the order book is handled by an exchange employee called an *order book official (OBO)*. If there is a discrepancy on a CBOE option trade, your broker will contact the OBO to resolve it.

For the most part, a covered call writer does not need to be overly concerned with the type of trading systems on the various exchanges. In almost all instances, it will be invisible to you. But there are slight differences that may become apparent if you are dealing with a fast-moving or relatively illiquid option. The biggest issue is that in a market-maker system, if you place a *limit order*—one specifying a price that must be met or bettered for execution to occur—the option can trade at your price without your order being filled if the trade is between market makers. This means that even if you see the option trade at your price after you have placed your order, it may not necessarily have been filled. If the option passes your price, then your order should be filled unless the print is from an earlier transaction out of sequence.

Options can trade on multiple exchanges and through multiple market makers. When you see an online quote, you are generally (though not always) looking at a *composite quote*, meaning the best bid and best offer from all available sources. However, when you enter an order, you do not know which exchange your brokerage firm's computer will direct it to or that it will always be to the exchange with the best price at the time. To illustrate, consider the following hypothetical scenario for quotes on a particular option.

Source	Bid	Offer
A	1.10	1.30
B	1.05	1.25
C	1.05	1.20
D	1.10	1.25

A composite quote for this option would show a bid of 1.10 and an offer of 1.20. A market order to buy *should* return an execution at 1.20. But if your order is routed to sources A, B, or D, you might get executed at 1.25 or 1.30. If you placed a limit order to buy at 1.20, that order should be executed immediately, but if your order doesn't go to source C, then it might not.

Sometimes, your quote source may be showing only one market's quote, not the composite quote. And you may be viewing quotes and trades that are delayed twenty minutes rather than real-time. Advice on placing orders will be found in Chapter 7, and suggestions on where to find real-time composite quotes will be found in Chapter 9.

All option exchanges have a procedure at the beginning of the day called the *opening rotation*. This was devised to help provide orderly markets in all of the options on a particular stock at the beginning of a trading session and to insure that all options open at a single price. (Listed stocks all open at a single price, though futures actually open in a range of prices.) The process operates in accordance with the following rules:

- Trading in the underlying stock must begin before any options on the stock can be traded. Thus, when a stock has a delayed opening or is halted during the day, option trading is suspended as well.
- Trading in each option on a given stock opens in an established order, with the farthest expiration months and lower strike prices opening first and the nearest expiration month and higher strike prices opening last.
- Once an opening trade (or quote) is established, no additional trades in that option can take place until trading on all other options on the same underlying security has opened.
- To be eligible as the opening transaction on any option, an order must be placed before the opening rotation.
- Public orders are given priority over those of market makers.

The rotation process is an efficient, orderly way of opening the markets on listed options, but it is not perfect. Even with the help of computers, it cannot be instantaneous, and orders received during the rotation cannot be processed until after the entire process is complete. Needless to say, the underlying stock can move significantly during this delay. Covered call writers should generally wait until a rotation is finished before initiating their orders.

Computerized Quotes

If you think the specialist for IBM stock on the NYSE has a tough job, consider that he has only a single security to worry about. By comparison, the market for IBM options at this writing has available both puts and calls in four different expiration months and seven different strike prices, for a total of fifty-six separate securities. And each of those options can change in price when the price of the underlying stock changes. Needless to say, bids and offers for options are now routinely updated by computer.

This may sound a little mechanical, but it's actually much better than the old way, which was manual and might have displayed a quote so old that it was nowhere near the current market. In those days (not really that long ago), you had to put in an option order you knew would be away from the market just to force the exchange floor to update the quote. Then, when you could see the updated quote, you would cancel your first order and replace it with one more likely to be executed. If the underlying stock moved in the meantime, you got into a futile game of cat and mouse with the floor.

Even though covered writing does not involve trading in and out of positions several times a day, understanding how executions work is important. With this knowledge, you will be better equipped to make the following assessments:

- when it is appropriate to use *market orders*, which are filled at the prevailing bids and offers, as opposed to limit orders
- at what price you can reasonably expect an execution
- whether the position is in your best interest or even meets your criteria

Liquidity

Liquidity refers to the trading activity in a listed security. It is of greater concern in dealing with options than with stocks. Liquid options trade actively; illiquid ones trade infrequently. There is no hard number that distinguishes the two, but if an option trades thousands of contracts per day, it is quite liquid; if it trades only a few or none at all, it is quite illiquid. If less than a few hundred contracts of a particular option trade on an average day, the spread between the bid and the offer will probably be very wide, a consideration in deciding whether to initiate a position in that option. If fewer than fifty contracts trade per day, the underlying stock should be particularly compelling or it may be wise to avoid it.

The issue is whether there is enough activity to get a good execution. The less liquid the option, generally the wider the spread and the more you will pay for a purchase (or the less you will receive from a sale) if you use market orders. On one position, a quarter of a point ($25 per contract) is generally not going to affect your annual returns in a material way. But on a bunch of trades over the year, it will. Admittedly, it's also a matter of principle. Most of the time, if you use limit orders and are a little patient, you can sell options somewhere between the quoted bid and offer or even sell at the offer. But with an illiquid option, you may have to sell at the bid, or risk having the stock move while you wait for a buyer to hit your limit price.

Along with average daily trading volume, you should also check the open interest when evaluating an option to sell. Open interest tells you how many outstanding contracts exist for any option, as of the previous night's close. It's helpful to see an open interest of more than one thousand options, although here, too, there is no magic number. If a stock has moved recently, you could be looking at a newly issued strike price that has almost no open interest at all yet. That does not mean you should necessarily avoid the option. It just tells you that it may be a bit more difficult to get it at the price you are interested in.

Recently, the option exchanges have begun posting *size* with each option quote, indicating how many option contracts can be executed at the stated bid or offer. For instance, if you see that 30 contracts of a particular call option are bid for at a particular price, you know that you can sell up to 30 at that price—regardless of volume or open interest considerations. It may be possible to sell *more* than 30, but you know you can sell at least 30. This figure is now available because of the electronic execution capabilities of the options market. When specialists or market makers place their markets in the electronic system, they must state how many contracts they are "good for" at the stated bid and ask prices. Consequently, size is now available to individuals, much as it has been for professional traders for a number of years.

RECAPPING JUST BEYOND THE BASICS

■ The money you pay or receive for an option is the *premium*. Option *prices* are quoted as per share amounts, while premiums are more frequently referred to in absolute dollar amounts. As an example, an option with a quoted price of 4.50 represents $450 in premium.

■ Option premiums are composed of *intrinsic* value and *time* value. Intrinsic value (also called *cash* value) is the amount, if any, by which an option is in the money—in other words, how much it would be worth right now if it were exercised, excluding commissions. For a call option, this value is determined by how far above the option's strike price the stock is trading. The time value component is simply that part of an option's premium over and above its intrinsic value.

■ The theoretical premium or value of an option is most often calculated using the *Black-Scholes formula*. The factors included in this formula are price of the underlying stock, strike price of the option, amount of time left until expiration, volatility of the underlying stock, any dividends paid, and the current interest rate. Though almost everyone uses the formula, different values will result from the fact that volatilities measured using different time periods can be used. *Volatility* is a measure of how far the underlying stock has moved, either up or down, in a given amount of time.

■ Options generally will be available in four different *expiration months:* the two nearest calendar months and the next two months in the quarterly cycle for the underlying stock. The *three quarterly cycles* are:

1 January-April-July-October

2 February-May-August-November

3 March-June-September-December

■ *Option symbols* are made up of three to five letters (depending on the stock symbol) and are created as follows: stock symbol (or "root") + one letter for option type and expiration + one letter for strike price.

■ Certain events can cause the option exchanges to *adjust* the terms of an option contract, even after you have bought or sold one. This action is decided upon by a joint adjustment panel of the option exchange and the OCC, and is taken only when necessary to make pre- and post-event positions equivalent. Regular cash dividends (those amounting to less than 10 percent of the value of the stock) are *not* considered sufficient to adjust the terms of an option. When an option has been adjusted from standard terms, it receives a different symbol.

■ Options on the Amex or Philadelphia exchanges trade by *specialist,* while the CBOE uses an exchange-based *market-maker system.* On all option exchanges, there is a procedure at the beginning of the day called the *opening rotation.* This creates an orderly market by providing a single opening transaction or quote for each option trading on a particular stock before allowing all of them to trade freely.

■ When evaluating an option to sell, you should check the average daily trading volume and the *open interest* to gauge its liquidity, as well as the bid and offer size. *Liquidity* will affect your ability to get a reasonable execution, or even your ability to get an execution at all at the price you want.

Covered Writing Mechanics   *3*

Clearly, the time has now come when the speculative stigma of options should be completely and irrevocably removed from the concept of writing covered options.

MAX ANSBACHER, president of Ansbacher Investment Management
and a successful options professional

CHAPTERS 1 AND 2 INTRODUCED THE FUNDAMENTAL CONCEPTS underlying options and their markets, as well as the principles and techniques involved in trading these instruments. This chapter explains how covered call writing combines a short position in a call option with a long position in a stock to form a new hybrid investment with unique profit and risk characteristics.

Combining stock with call options in this manner is a conservative technique that has been utilized since before options were even listed on formal exchanges. In fact, options were first introduced by stock owners who offered call options on their individual holdings through newspaper ads. Since becoming listed securities, call options have been used by portfolio managers to reduce the risk in stock portfolios of institutions such as insurance companies, endowments, and pension funds. Unfortunately, it was formerly difficult for individual investors to take advantage of the technique. Access to real-time option prices was limited or very expensive, and transaction costs all but negated the benefits for small investors. All that has now

41

changed, with the advent of discount brokerages and online access to stock and option data through the Internet. Now, covered call writing represents a viable investment technique for just about any stock investor who is willing to take the time to learn what it's all about.

REQUIREMENTS FOR "VALID" COVERED WRITES

As noted above, covered call writing involves the sale of call options against shares of stock held in one's account. Call options of any available expiration month and strike price may be sold to create a covered write. The combined position can be of any size (100 shares and 1 contract, 2,500 shares and 25 contracts, 25,000 shares and 250 contracts, and so on), and the two parts may be initiated simultaneously, or call options can be sold on a stock position already in your portfolio. To be deemed a valid covered write by your brokerage firm for margin purposes, the two component positions must exhibit the following characteristics:

- **Both the stock and the options must be in the same account.** You may not, for example, have the stock in your individual retirement account and write the call in your regular account.
- **The stock held must be the underlying security specified by the short option or a security that can be converted into the underlying, such as a warrant or another option.** If you are going to write a call on ABC stock, you could have twenty other stocks in your account, worth far more than 100 ABC, but your ABC call would still be considered naked unless you are long 100 ABC in the account. (Covered writing against warrants or options will be discussed in Chapter 7.)
- **You must hold at least enough shares of stock to fulfill the delivery requirement of the call option.** Unless otherwise adjusted, each call option represents 100 shares of the underlying stock. Therefore, if you sell 5 calls, anything less than 500 shares would leave one or more of those calls uncovered. Having more than the requisite number of shares to deliver if assigned is not a problem.

These criteria are not just academic. They determine whether you will be subject to a margin requirement or, in some cases, whether you will be permitted to maintain such a position in your account. Only fully covered option positions, for example, are permitted in cash or retirement accounts.

RISK/REWARD OF A COVERED WRITE

Although they show as two separate positions in your account, the two parts of a covered write effectively form a new hybrid position that offers risk/reward characteristics different from those of either of its components. This is illustrated in figure 3-1.

Figure 3-1   Basic Risk/Reward for Components of a Covered Write

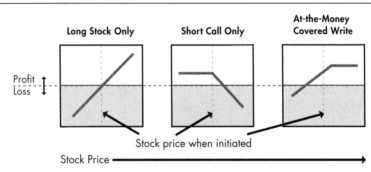

A long position in XYZ stock by itself has dollar-for-dollar opportunity on the upside as well as dollar-for-dollar risk on the downside. In other words, every dollar rise or fall in the stock price represents a dollar gain or loss for the investor. While your gain on a stock position is theoretically unlimited, the maximum loss is whatever you paid for the shares. A short call position with no accompanying stock position is naked and highly risky. Its maximum gain equals the net premium received from the sale of the call, and its loss is theoretically unlimited should the price of XYZ shares rise substantially. That's because, in order to deliver the shares represented by the option if it's exercised, you would have to buy them in the market. So the higher the stock's price rises above the strike, the more you would be out of pocket.

A simple at-the-money covered write (option strike = current stock price) reduces the downside risk of the stock alone and completely eliminates the upside risk of the short call. The cost of the stock position is reduced by the amount of the premium earned from selling the call. This lowers your break-even point—the share price at which you neither gain nor lose money—and also reduces your maximum potential loss. Since you don't have to go to the market to fill an assignment on the short call, you've eliminated the risk posed to the naked call writer by a strong move upward in the stock.

The trade-off for the reduced risk of the covered write is a limited upside potential. An at-the-money covered write has a potential upside equal to the amount of option premium received. The potential upside of an out-of-the-money covered write stems from both the option premium and any gain in the stock, up to the strike price. By varying the strike price of the call option, covered writers can balance potential gain against risk reduction to suit their objectives. In addition, the covered call will realize at least some profit over a wider range of stock prices than either component by itself.

Now consider the following example of positions initiated two months before option expiration:

Long 100 XYZ at $48
Short 1 XYZ Nov 50 call at 2

Figure 3-2 plots the returns at expiration for the covered write combining the two positions above against those from a long position in the stock alone. It shows that, while giving up some of the potential upside enjoyed by the stockholder, the covered writer enjoys a better return for all stock prices up to $52 during the period. If the stock price is below $50 (the strike) at expiration, the gain on the covered call exceeds the stock return by 2 points, the amount of the option premium. Once the stock price reaches $50, the difference narrows until the share price reaches $52, the strike price plus the amount of the option premium. At a share price of $52, the covered write and the stock generate the same return; for all prices above that, the stock gain is greater. Thus, $52 is the "crossover" price for the two strategies.

Figure 3-2 Covered Write versus Long Stock

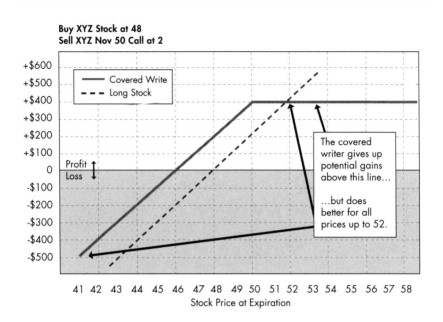

The following table summarizes the profit/loss characteristics of all three of the positions from the example:

	Long Stock (Alone)	Short Option (Alone)	Covered Write
Maximum Gain	Unlimited	2	4
Maximum Loss	48	Unlimited	46
Break-even Stock Price	48 (Losses start below this price)	52 (Losses start above this price)	46 (Losses start below this price)

Risk/Reward Characteristics Over Time

The illustrations above can be found in many texts on options. They are helpful for understanding the basic risk/reward characteristics of buying stock and selling a covered call option, but they fall short of describing the risk/reward features of covered writing as an ongoing investment practice. They are valid only for the time the option exists and thus ignore the fact that risk/reward characteristics for covered writes can be modified over time.

When you buy stock, your risk/reward remains constant until you dispose of it. That could be a day, a month, or ten years. It doesn't matter how long the holding period is or where the stock goes during that time. If you buy the stock at $48, as in the above example, and it goes to $120 in six months, you have an unrealized gain of 72 points, but unless you sell it, your break-even on the initial investment and your potential gain or loss do not change. Thus, if the stock turns around and goes back down to $25 in the following six months (a common occurrence during the past few years) and you sell it at that point, you will still have lost nearly half your original investment.

Assume instead that you initiate the above covered write in XYZ, and at option expiration in November, the stock is trading at 49. The November 50 call expires worthless, but you still own the stock. You might now be able to write a January 50 call at 2. What happens if you do that? You reduce your maximum loss, lower your breakeven, and raise your maximum gain by the amount of the new premium—to $44, $44, and $6 per share, respectively. So, you start out by initiating a position that has less risk (although also less profit potential) than owning the stock by itself. Then, a couple of months later, you take in more option premium, reducing your risk even more and adding to your profit potential. This scenario, pictured in figure 3-3, illustrates how multiple writes on the same stock position further reduce its risk and boost its gains. Thus, covered writing enables investors, *over time*, to approximate the returns of owning stock but with less risk.

Of course, the stock will not always be accommodating enough to remain flat, giving you a chance to write a second call with the same strike price. However, regardless of whether the stock price goes up or down after the covered write is initiated, there are follow-up actions that the investor can take to reduce risk, lower the breakeven, or increase the upside potential of the original covered write. Unfortunately, you cannot create a graph of the risk/reward for multiple covered writes over a long period because there would be an infinite number of scenarios and follow-up actions to consider. But you *can*

Figure 3-3   Changes to Risk/Reward for Second Covered Write

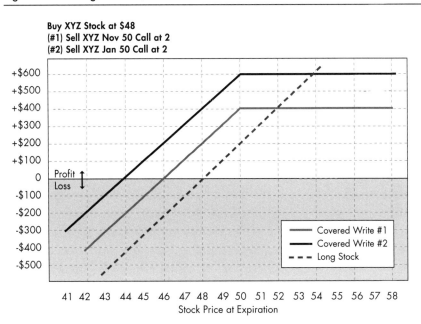

Buy XYZ Stock at $48
(#1) Sell XYZ Nov 50 Call at 2
(#2) Sell XYZ Jan 50 Call at 2

examine how any *specific* follow-up action will alter the risk/reward of an existing position, as shown above. This will be discussed further in the next chapter.

Risk Transference

Call buyers provide the fuel for the covered writing engine by purchasing, for a limited period of time, the upside potential of a particular stock beyond a specified stock price. The appeal of buying a call is, of course, the ability to enjoy substantial upside potential with a limited investment and consequently a limited potential loss. The leverage can be huge. When Microsoft was trading at $58, you could, for example, have purchased an eight-month call option at the 60 strike price for 6.6, or $660. That call would give you a stake in the upside potential of Microsoft stock over the next two-thirds of a year for a little more than 10 percent of what it would cost to own a round lot of the stock itself—$5,800. At the same time, the call buyer's total risk is $660, while the stock owner's risk is technically the entire $5,800.

The call buyer knows that the process will lose money frequently, if not most of the time. That's because, for the position to gain, the stock must not only go up but must go beyond the call buyer's break-even point—the strike price plus the call premium ($66.6 in the Microsoft example)—by expiration. In reality, call buyers do not generally hold their calls until expiration, preferring to take short-term profits if the underlying stock moves in their favor. Regardless of whether they hold to expiration, however, they hope that over time even a few substantial gains will offset the losses they know they will also sustain.

Call writers take the opposite side of this game. They reap a series of small, consistent returns as time value dwindles away on the call options they sell. Since covered writers own the underlying stock, they have complete protection from upside loss on the call option, incurring only an opportunity loss when the stock goes up. They do, of course, still have the downside risk of the stock itself.

Covered writers are thus stockholders who, for a given period, would rather have a known income received immediately than an uncertain upside. This income is the owner's to keep regardless of the stock's price movements. As such, it will always mitigate the downside risk in the stock position during the period. Covered writers know that the upside potential of the strategy is not as great as holding the stock by itself for the same period, but they also know that the option premiums will provide a greater return than simply owning the stock when the stock price goes down or remains flat.

Shorting a Call versus Shorting a Stock

From the above discussion, it should be clear that, although covered writing involves a short option position, it is very different from shorting a stock. For the investing naïve, selling a stock short, which involves selling shares you don't own, is practically synonymous with risk and speculation. Some fear that if enough short sellers "gang up" on a particular stock, their combined willpower can actually make the stock drop in value. Part of this stigma has been transferred to covered writes, but that is completely unjustified: When you short (or write) a covered option, you are merely selling someone the right to buy stock you already hold; you are not *selling* something you do not own. And significantly, when you short a call against an existing stock position, you still have a *bullish* position: You would much rather have the stock go up than down. So covered writing is not at all like shorting a stock. (If you do not own the stock and are selling the call naked, that is a different story.)

Here's a quick comparison between shorting stock and calls:

Shorting a Stock	Shorting a Covered Call
Is bearish—you need the stock to go down to make money	Is neutral to bullish—you need the stock to remain where it is or go up to make money
Has theoretically unlimited risk if the stock goes up	Makes money and suffers only an opportunity loss when the stock goes up. (If the option is closed at a loss at expiration, that loss would be offset by a similar gain in the stock.)
Involves selling stock you do not own, which requires your broker to borrow shares for you to sell	Involves a commitment to sell something you already own, with no borrowing of any kind required
Requires margin	Does not require margin
Must be initiated on an uptick in the stock—that is, at a price higher than the last one at which the stock traded	Has no uptick rule

More on Exercise and Assignment

As noted in Chapter 1, an option holder can exercise anytime before expiration. That means a covered call writer can receive an assignment at any time. This may seem like a concern, but in reality it is not. In fact, it is generally *good news* for a writer to be assigned before expiration—it accelerates, and therefore increases, his or her return. It is like having your bank send you all your maturing certificate of deposit principal and interest before it is due. The only time it is really undesirable is when you are selling calls against a stock that you would not want called away (for tax purposes or some other reason), and this discussion will help you prevent that.

While calls *can* be assigned at any time, they will not be unless or until it is in a holder's interest to exercise. The key, therefore, to determining when an early exercise is likely to occur is to understand the benefits of doing so from a holder's perspective. Call holders are generally speculating that the price of the underlying stock will rise enough to create a profit on the option before it expires. But what they really want is not to exercise the option but to close out for a profit before expiration. They rarely buy calls as a means of acquiring a stock, and they don't want to incur the additional commissions involved in exercising and selling the shares. It is therefore seldom in a call buyer's interest to exercise before expiration. This is certainly the case when the option is out of the money (to buy shares of stock via exercise at $45 when it's selling in the open market for $35 is obviously absurd, regardless of what one may have originally paid for the option).

But what about when the stock rises and pushes the option into the money? Say your option is the 45 call and the stock is now trading at $50. Theoretically, you could exercise and immediately sell the stock, thereby capturing the 5 points of intrinsic, or cash, value. But options tend to carry some amount of time value right up until the last few days or hours before expiration, even when they are somewhat in the money. And as long as a call option has time value (regardless of whether it is profitable or not), a holder will always receive more money by selling it than by exercising and selling the stock.

Example:
DEF stock is trading at $53
DEF Aug 50 calls are trading at 3.75

If you held the DEF call, you would be unwise to exercise, even though it is in the money. Why? The option does have 3.00 of cash value, but it also has 0.75 of time value that you would give up by exercising. You would be better off selling the call at 3.75 and buying the stock in the market at $53. That way, you would end up with a net cost of $49.25 a share for the stock, compared with $50 if you exercised. (In reality, you would also consider commissions in determining whether exercising is worthwhile.)

Note: The price you paid for the call is irrelevant to this discussion. Regardless of whether you currently have a profit or a loss on the position, you are better off selling the option than exercising it while it still has time value (unless your transaction costs will eat up that value).

What are the implications for the covered writer? There is very little chance of an early exercise while the option contains any time value. So if you are at all concerned about being assigned, check on whether the option is trading with time value. If it is in the money and has at least 0.50 in time value, it is very unlikely to be exercised. If it has only 0.05 to 0.10 of time value, or if the bid price is lower than its cash value (for example, if the option in the above example were bid at 2.90 when the stock was trading at $53), then you might be assigned early. One factor that can sometimes lead to early assignments is an impending cash dividend. Occasionally, holders will exercise in time to own the stock on the record day for the dividend, but again, this will not likely happen until the option trades very close to parity (with no time value).

At expiration, if a stock is trading right at the strike price, assignments may or may not occur. If in the above example, DEF closes on the Friday before expiration at exactly $50, the writer may or may not be assigned or may receive a partial assignment. It is not uncommon to receive an assignment notice on only part of your position. You may, for example, have 1,000 shares of stock and 10 short call options and receive notice of assignment on 300 shares.

The only scenario that can be even more beneficial to you as a covered writer than being assigned is to have your stock end up right at the strike price on expiration and *not* be assigned. If that occurs, you realize the maximum gain on the stock for the period, yet you still own the stock. You do not incur the transaction costs of being assigned and purchasing another stock, and you should be able to get an attractive at-the-money premium for the following month to write another call on your shares.

CALCULATING POTENTIAL RETURNS

Because the call options in a covered write have both a defined life and a maximum potential gain (the premium you took in from their sale), it is relatively easy to project a rate of return for the position at various price points for the underlying stock at expiration. Most commonly, writers will look at returns for two key prices: the strike price of the option and the current price of the stock. Since this is handily accomplished by a computer for all potential covered writes on all optionable stocks, covered writers can quickly compare the risks and potential rewards of different writes on the same stock or of writes on numerous different stocks, even as prices change during the day. (Chapter 9 discusses some of the Internet-based services for covered writers that provide such comparisons.)

Return if Exercised (RIE)

The maximum reward potential for a covered write occurs when the stock is above the strike price at expiration and the option is exercised. When calculating this potential, the return is frequently referred to as the *return if exercised* (RIE), or *return if assigned* or *return if called*. The RIE, which can be expressed either as a raw (absolute) return for the period until expiration or as an annualized return, is simply the potential gain in the stock (up to the strike price) plus the option premium received.

Consider again the example used earlier:

Buy 100 XYZ at $48
Sell 1 XYZ Nov 50 call at 2

Assume that the positions are initiated two months before option expiration and that transaction costs are excluded.

$$\textbf{Raw RIE} \quad = \quad \frac{\text{call premium received + potential gain in the stock}}{\text{initial investment in the stock}}$$

$$= \frac{\$100 \times [\text{premium} + (\text{strike price} - \text{initial stock price})]}{\text{initial stock price}}$$

$$= \frac{\$200 + (\$5,000 - 4,800)}{\$4,800}$$

$$= \frac{\$400}{\$4,800}$$

$$= \mathbf{8.33\%}$$

(Note: If this were an in-the-money covered write, strike price minus stock price would be a negative number.)

Annualized $= \dfrac{\text{Raw RIE} \times 365}{\text{\# days till expiration}}$
RIE

$$= \frac{0.0833 \times 365}{60}$$

$$= \mathbf{50.67\%}$$

It is not uncommon to project annualized returns from covered writes at this level when writing out-of-the-money calls. Remember, however, that this is the best-case scenario and that the annualized projection further assumes that you can get an equivalent return on other writes during the remainder of the year. It is therefore unrealistic to project annual performance based on the formula's results for a single covered write. Annualized RIE is very helpful, though, as a basis for comparing or ranking different covered writing opportunities, since it equalizes the time period in all cases. (Examples of how one can compare covered writes by their annualized returns are presented in Chapter 9.)

Return Unchanged

A secondary (and more conservative) calculation is also generally made on potential covered writes based on the assumption that at option expiration the underlying stock is trading at its present price. The result of this calculation is commonly referred to as the *return unchanged* (RU), or the *static* or *flat return.*

For an out-of-the-money covered write, like the one in our example, assuming no change in the share price means the potential gain in the stock will be zero.

$$\textbf{Raw RU} \quad = \quad \frac{\text{call premium received} + \text{potential gain in the stock}}{\text{initial investment in the stock}}$$

$$= \quad \frac{2+0}{48}$$

$$= \quad \textbf{4.17\%}$$

(Note: For an in-the-money covered write, the RIE and the RU are equal, since the stock would be called away at expiration in either scenario.)

$$\textbf{Annualized RU} \quad = \quad \frac{\text{Raw RU} \times 365}{\text{number of days until expiration}}$$

$$= \quad \frac{0.0417 \times 365}{60}$$

$$= \quad \textbf{25.37\%}$$

Return Based on Net Debit

Since covered writes can be initiated with a single transaction or at least in the same day, your brokerage account will be debited for the stock at the same time that it is credited with the option premium. The resulting charge to your account for the two items combined can therefore be considered a *net debit* that represents the actual money invested. In the above example, since you bought stock at $48 and sold a call for 2, your account would be debited $4,800 plus transaction costs for the stock and credited $200 less transaction costs for the option. This results in a net debit to your account of $4,600. Thus, it would be valid to view your initial investment as the stock price less the option premium. Looking at the option premium this way (as a reduction of your initial investment), rather than as part of your ultimate returns, results in slightly higher calculated rates of returns (the absolute return remains the same) for covered writes, since the initial investment is smaller. In the example above, the raw RIE would be 8.7 percent if calculated this way, rather than 8.3 percent, and the annualized RIE 52.9 percent, rather than 50.7 percent. The difference can be much more dramatic for lower-priced stocks or in-the-money writes where the option premium is larger. This book will use the more conservative calculations based on the full stock price, unless otherwise noted.

EXECUTING THE STRATEGY

ARMED WITH A BASIC KNOWLEDGE OF OPTIONS AND THE WAY COVered calls work with stock holdings, you are now in a position to appreciate how covered writing can become an ongoing investment strategy and what it can do for you. Part Two will take you from the development of a call writing strategy to the creation of realistic expectations and on into implementation. Along the way, you'll get examples, supporting data, tips, "how to's," and a list of tools available to covered writers. What is even more important, you will gain new insights into a powerful technique that can change the way you invest.

Turning a Position into a Strategy 4

If you don't profit from your investment mistakes, someone else will.

YALE HIRSCH, publisher of the *Stock Trader's Almanac*

STOCK INVESTING CAN BE SIMPLE OR COMPLEX, DEPENDING ON your approach. Covered call writing is no different. It may seem that covered writing involves a lot of details, but it can be rewarding and successful at any level of complexity. In this, it's like sailing. Almost anyone can take a 14-foot sailboat out in calm waters and, with minimal knowledge, have a safe and enjoyable experience. If you want to expand your horizons, you can learn how to race, how to negotiate rough weather, or how to handle a much more complex boat. It's up to you. But you don't have to reject the idea of sailing altogether because you are intimidated by the prospect of taking a 40-foot, twin-masted schooner on a five-day offshore cruise by yourself; you just have to lower your threshold of enjoyment a little. The same goes for covered call writing. Through the selection of the underlying stock to buy and the particular call option to write, the strategy can be tailored to a multitude of different risk levels and market conditions, as well as a variety of goals and approaches. This chapter will discuss the various uses covered writing can be put to and the ways it can be modified to suit various circumstances.

A New Way of Thinking

If you sell a call option on stock you own, you will have created a covered write. But at that point you will have done little more than add a new investment position to your account. When your thinking has changed so that you continually look for opportunities to sell covered calls, and when option writing is an ongoing activity that affects the make-up and performance of your portfolio, then you will have yourself a new investment strategy.

In the process of creating a covered write, you will discover that it alters not just the risk/reward parameters of your stock investment but the *way* you invest as well—your selection process, your expectations, and your follow-up activities. The change in your thinking and the implementation of follow-up activities are what will turn a position in your account into an ongoing investment strategy. A discussion of these activities follows. A diagram of how they create an ongoing strategy is found in figure 4-1 at right.

Follow-up Actions

You may feel that it is not necessary to monitor a covered write as closely as a stock position by itself, and that is generally true. However, you should remember that the option has a limited life and that you will need to take follow-up action at some point. Follow-up actions can be taken at any time, even before the option expires, and may be warranted if the stock moves sharply or if you have reason to believe it *may* do so. Such follow-up actions will be discussed below, but first consider the simple case—the one where you do nothing until expiration.

The Simple Case: Doing Nothing until Expiration

Once you put on a covered write, you need not take any further action, even at expiration. You can do absolutely nothing—you don't even need to be around. You can be in Tahiti on expiration day if you want. There is nothing about a covered write that adds any more risk than if you simply owned the stock.

Figure 4-1   Covered Writing as an Ongoing Strategy

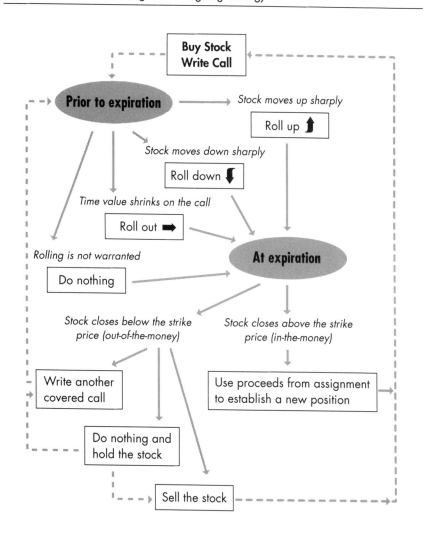

Just remember that at expiration, the option will do one of two things: expire worthless or be exercised. If the option is exercised, your stock will be called away, and your broker will deposit funds in your account. On the other hand, if the call expires worthless, you will revert to your status as a simple stockholder.

If you do not reinvest the proceeds of an assignment or write another call in a timely fashion, you are not really embracing covered writing as an ongoing strategy and are not taking advantage of its ongoing benefits. If you are frequently leaving non-invested funds from assignments in your account, perhaps you should consider a different investment approach.

While being assigned provides the maximum gain for the period, having calls expire worthless is also gratifying, because you know you have done better for the period than someone who simply owned the stock. What's more, you are now free to write another option and take in still more premium.

Closing Part or All of the Position

Once you begin writing covered calls on a regular basis, you will discover numerous reasons why you might want to close or modify a position before expiration. News affecting the stock may become public, or you may need the money for something. Or you may simply wake up one morning and ask yourself, "What was I thinking?" The reason is irrelevant. The ability to adjust your position on the fly is one of the great benefits of covered writing. One alternative is to close out part or all of your position. You can do this whenever you want, provided you have not received an assignment notice on any of your calls. Of course, in closing, you will incur transaction costs and may realize a loss on one or both sides of the transaction, so you do not want to make a habit of it. But when the necessity arises, the ability to close is there.

Say that in September you buy ABC stock at $32 and sell a Jan 35 call for 3 points, for a net investment of $29 a share (not including transaction costs). Then in October, the stock falls to $27. You believe it could drop farther and would like to prevent further risk, but your call option still has nearly three months until expiration and is trading at 1.5. Closing would leave you with net proceeds of $25.5 a share ($27 for selling the stock, minus $1.5 for buying the offsetting call). That gives you a loss of $3.5 per share (the initial net investment of $29 minus $25.5), plus transaction costs, on the covered write (compared with a $5 per share loss had you simply owned the stock and not written a call). If you believe that the stock could go to $20 or below over the next three months, then holding on to a short call that will only give you $1.50 more profit during that time may not make sense. Closing the whole position in that scenario is a justifiable action.

The important point to remember is that your net investment incorporates both the stock and the call option, but the stock contributes essentially *all* the downside risk. Therefore, it behooves you to assess where you believe the stock may go even more than where the option may go and not to be shy about closing the option or both sides if necessary.

Another tactic many people fail to appreciate is closing only part of the position. If you have 800 shares of a stock and write 8 calls, you can always compromise by closing only four of the options. For some reason, people get stuck on the idea that it's all or none and don't think of simply lightening their position rather than closing it entirely. The same holds true for putting on the position in the first place. Not sure if you should sell a covered call on all 800 shares? Why not sell only 4, or sell 4 at a conservative strike price and 4 at a higher one?

One caution on closing covered writes: You'd be very ill advised to close the stock and keep the short call position open, even if you are trying to avoid taking a loss on the option. Whether or not you are approved for naked options, it is an unwise practice to close a covered write by selling the stock first and holding an uncovered short position in the call.

Rolling Options

You will probably not need to close a covered write unless something dramatic enough happens to make you get out of the stock entirely. More often, you will decide to *roll* your call position. *Rolling* refers to the process of closing out the short call position in a covered write and opening a new one in its place. Think of it as simply substituting different calls for the ones you are currently short. This allows you to adjust the risk/reward potential of your position while leaving the stock holding intact.

The act of rolling involves both a purchase (to close your original short position) and a sale (to establish a new short position). You will generally want to execute the two transactions as closely together as possible, to minimize the risk of having the stock move between the time you execute one side and the time you execute the other. Even though the stock *could* move in a direction favorable to the second half of your transaction after you've completed the first half (giving you a better price), why take that risk? Your objective is to have a covered write, not to day trade options. Therefore, rolling is normally accomplished either in two nearly simultaneous transactions or as a single transaction executed as a "spread" order. (Executing such trades will be discussed in more detail in Chapter 8.)

Having said that, there may be occasions when you wish to close your short call position and not reopen a new one at the same time. You could, for example, write a call option against stock and subsequently find out that another company may be interested in acquiring the one you own stock in. Rather than cap your upside with a covered call, you may decide to close the short call position and wait a week or two to see if your stock rises or any news comes out. (Before you do, however, read the section below on covered writing for hot stocks.)

Rolling is a valuable technique, allowing you to manage the risk and reward of your covered writes *after* you have initiated them. However, it has a price. It will add transaction costs and can sometimes require additional funds to implement. Furthermore, it will not always end up being a better course of action than having done nothing. As with changing course on any investment decision, your success is ultimately a product of the accuracy of your judgments.

Below is a discussion of how and when it might be appropriate to roll options up, down, or out. The following example will be used throughout:

Buy 100 DEF at $28
Sell 1 Feb 30 call at 2
Days to expiration = 60

Rolling Up

Suppose you buy DEF at $28 and write the DEF Feb 30 call at 2 in December. Suppose further that it is now January, and DEF is trading at $32 and looking strong. The covered write is working well, and you have an unrealized gain at this point: Your call is worth 3, netting you a potential $29 per share before transaction costs should you close both positions now. If the stock remains above $30 at February's expiration, you will achieve your maximum gain from the initial covered write. You can certainly opt to do nothing and wait for that to happen.

But you may feel that the stock could move even higher over the next month. If you are that confident, you can adjust your position to allow you more upside potential by rolling up to the Feb 35 calls. The following pricing scenario exists.

Original Scenario Two Months to Expiration	New Scenario One Month to Expiration
DEF = $28	DEF = $32
DEF Feb 35 Call = 0.5	DEF Feb 35 Call = 1
DEF Feb 30 Call = 2	DEF Feb 30 Call = 3
DEF Feb 25 Call = 4.25	DEF Feb 25 Call = 7.3

Rolling up to the Feb 35 call would involve buying the Feb 30 call to close your current position and selling the Feb 35 call to establish a new covered write. Since you are paying 3 points and receiving 1, you are paying out 2 points net, or $200 per contract. This payment is your net debit for the transaction and represents an addition to the initial cost of the investment. This cost happens to cancel out the 2 points earned on the original option write, so, in a sense, it is giving back the premium. Depending on how much time remains before expiration and how high the stock has moved, your net cost to roll up could be more or less what you originally received. (None of this includes transaction costs.)

Why would you do this? The logic would be that you are increasing your upside potential, although you are also adding to your original investment and thereby increasing your risk. Your original position gained a maximum of 4 points at expiration if exercised (30 for your stock + 2 from the option – your net initial investment on the stock of 28). Your new position now gains a maximum of 7 points if exercised (35 for the stock + 0 from options – your investment of 28). Your break-even point is higher now, and your time period is unchanged.

The comparison of risk/reward looks like this:

Rolling Up

	Original Scenario	New Scenario
Premium received (in points)	2	2 – 3 + 1 = 0
Maximum potential stock gain (strike price less initial stock price)	30 – 28 = 2	35 – 28 = 7
Total potential gain from stock and options	4	7
Break-even stock price (initial stock price less premium earned)	$26	$28
Time period	Feb expiration	Feb expiration

One way to decide whether this is worth doing is to look at your incremental investment and incremental gain. Here, you are putting in an extra $200 for an increase in your maximum potential gain of $300. That would be more than 100 percent on your incremental investment if realized, although when you figure in your transaction costs, it will be somewhat less. But what is the probability that the stock will actually be over $35 by February's expiration? That's for you to decide.

A little rough arithmetic tells you that the original covered write makes 4 points if the stock is above $30, while the new scenario makes 4 points if the stock is above $32 at expiration. Therefore, if the share price is below $32, you will have been better off not rolling, and if it is higher than $32, your roll will have been beneficial. (If you do this kind of quick math, you might want to toss in an extra half point for the transaction costs.)

Rolling Up and Out

Many people like the idea of rolling up for more potential gain on a covered write position but not the part about putting in additional capital. That's where *rolling up and out* comes in. You roll up but also move out to a more distant expiration month. By moving out in time, it is frequently possible to get more premium from your new write than it will cost to buy back your existing one. In other words, you will be rolling for a *net credit* rather than for a *net debit*.

Suppose you wish to roll up to the 35 strike price on your DEF calls, but you want more premium than is available in the Feb 35 call. Try March. Say the March 35 call is 2.25. That's a reasonable roll, but it will still cost you 0.75 points, or $75, per contract to do it. Assume there is an April 35 call at 3.5. This roll would give you a credit of 0.50, or $50, per contract. The April 35 call would extend your covered write two more months, so you want to be sure that you are considering this fact in your evaluation.

Rolling Up and Out

	Original Scenario	New Scenario
Premium received *(points)*	2	2 – 3 + 3.5 = **2.5**
Maximum potential stock gain (strike price less initial stock price)	30 – 28 = 2	35 – 28 = **7**
Total potential gain from stock and options	4	**9.5**
Break-even stock price (initial stock price less premium earned)	$26	$25.5
Time period	Feb expiration	Apr expiration

Many covered writers will not roll an option position unless they can do so for a credit. That is not a bad rule. By taking in additional premium, you will always be lowering your risk. However, if getting a credit requires that you write a new option more than five to seven months away, you may want to think twice. If you would not ordinarily consider selling a particular call against your stock position, then don't roll out to that call, either.

Rolling Down

As you might expect, *rolling down* is a more defensive follow-up action. Suppose that instead of rising, DEF drops to $25 in January. If you are afraid that it might fall further in the next month, you can close the whole position and absorb your loss, or you can roll your option down to the Feb 25 calls. When you drop to a lower strike price, you should always be able to receive a credit, since the lower strike price will inevitably have more premium than the one you are covering. (If for some strange reason, it does not, then you would gain nothing from the move.)

The rationale for rolling down would be that the stock has declined and you are willing to give up some additional upside potential in order to protect your position more on the downside. Assuming that the Feb 25 call can be sold for 2 and the Feb 30 call purchased for 0.35, you can take in another 1.65 credit, or $165 per contract. The comparison looks like this.

Rolling Down

	Original Scenario	New Scenario
Premium received (in points)	2	2 – 0.35 + 2 = **3.65**
Potential gain from stock (strike price less initial stock price)	30 – 28 = 2	25 – 28 = –3
Total potential gain from stock and options	**4**	**0.65**
Break-even stock price (initial stock price less premium earned)	**$26**	**$24.35**
Time period	Feb expiration	Feb expiration

You will now have removed almost all of your upside but will have lowered your break-even point. As with the scenario above, you could also *roll down and out* by going to the March 25 or even April 25 call for slightly more premium. Rolling down and out, however, is still defensive: It caps or reduces any potential from a gain in the stock, yet still contains downside risk. In fact, one danger in rolling down is that you may lock in a loss on the stock if, as in the example, the new strike price is below the price at which you originally bought the shares and you are assigned. If you are that bearish on the prospects for a particular stock, you might be better off closing the original covered write altogether or just rolling down within the current month to see what happens in the short term.

Rolling Out

Rolling out has less to do with movement in the stock than with time. The most common situation in which you would do this is when you are approaching expiration and the stock is close to the strike price, whether just below or just above. Assume it is now the Friday morning before February expiration (the last trading day) and DEF is trading at $29.95. The Feb 30 call might sell for 0.15 at this point. If the stock closes under $30, the option will expire worthless, and you could look to write the March or April 30 call on Monday. But the stock could just as easily close at $30.25, in which case you would be assigned and your stock called away. On Monday, you would have to buy the stock back or look for another position.

Now, you may be ready to jettison DEF from your portfolio, in which case you are hoping it does get called away. In that case, no action is necessary. If, on the other hand, you like DEF and plan to write another call on it anyway, you could roll the option out to March and not worry about whether it closes above or below $30, or whether it opens higher or lower on Monday. Assuming you were planning to write the March call anyway, the additional cost of this move is the $15 per contract you must pay to close the Feb 30 call, plus the transaction cost. When rolling out at the same strike price, you will always take in more money than you spend, because the more distant option will inevitably have more time value. So you will be receiving money (rolling for a credit), but you should still view the cost of the purchase as an added expense, since it will reduce what you receive from the new call you write. It may not seem like much to buy back a call for $15, but if you did that enough times during the year, it could add up.

Your approach would be similar if the stock was trading slightly above the strike, at, say, $30.25, even several days before expiration.

If you plan to hold the stock and write the March 30 call at expiration anyway, then you could roll out to the next month at this point instead of waiting for expiration.

- **Rolling:** The process of closing the short call position in a covered write and opening (substituting) a different covered call position on the same stock
- **Rolling up:** Substituting a call with a higher strike price
- **Rolling down:** Substituting a call with a lower strike price
- **Rolling out:** Substituting a call with a more distant expiration
- **Spread order:** A single order that involves both a purchase and a sale of options of the same type on the same stock for a specified "net" price. By accepting such an order, your brokerage firm guarantees that both sides will be executed together as long as your net price can be met. Otherwise nothing is done. Covered writers frequently use spread orders to roll their option positions.
- **Net price:** The combined price of a two-sided transaction involving the purchase and sale of either two options or a stock and an option.
  - —(*Net credit*) If the price of the sell side is greater than the price of the buy side, then the result is a net credit.
  - —(*Net debit*) If the price of the purchase is greater, then the result is a net debit.

Other Considerations

Thus far, the discussion on rolling assumes that you are in a fully covered write and that you roll to a similar position by selling the same number of new calls as you were previously short. This will be the most frequent case, but you can roll for fewer or more contracts if you desire (although if you write more than you have shares to support, the extras are not covered). Say you have 1,000 shares of a stock and have written 10 covered calls and decide to roll them. Whether you are rolling up, down, or out, you may decide to write only 7 calls, particularly if you can still get a credit for doing so. Similarly, if you were not fully covered to begin with—you had written only 5 calls, say, on your 1,000 shares—you could roll those 5 into, say, 7 or even 10 new ones to cover your cost. The latter strategy is called *partial writing* and will be discussed further in Chapter 8.

When judiciously implemented, rolling adds a tremendous amount of flexibility to covered writing, but too much of a good thing can be dangerous. If you are continually rolling positions, it may be appropriate to reconsider your original parameters for initiating covered writes. Some people, for example, will put on a covered write with a stock at $29.50 and sell the 30 strike call; then, as soon as the stock goes over $30, they look to roll. This will threaten the advantages of the strategy by adding unnecessary transaction costs over time.

COVERED CALL STRATEGIES

Flexibility is unquestionably one of the hallmarks of covered call writing. If you own stock and are not writing options, things are black or white—you either hold your shares or you sell them. Covered call writing expands your follow-up possibilities to include a number of ways to hedge the stock, in terms of both the amount and the time period. It also enables you to adjust the risk/reward parameters of your positions, should either the stock price or the market conditions warrant it. This flexibility expands dramatically over time, since you can write new options once the initial ones expire, or you can roll an existing position up or down or out before expiration. In this manner, you can control how much or how little of the total potential return you give up on the stock in exchange for a fixed premium, and you can change this amount each time a new call is written. From this perspective, a covered writer can actually use the options to *drive* the returns on the underlying stock position.

Because of its flexibility, covered writing can be implemented in different ways, to achieve a number of investment objectives. The following will be discussed in this section:

- incremental call writing on existing stock positions
- partially hedging, or reducing the downside risk on specific stock positions

- ▪ lessening risk in a portfolio too small to diversify
- ▪ participating in "hot" stocks, with lower risk and volatility
- ▪ exiting a long-held stock
- ▪ deferring capital gains taxes

The emphasis, however, will be on using continuous covered call writing as a primary investment strategy to generate an attractive total return, with a portfolio specifically designed for that purpose. This is the *total return*, or *buy-write*, approach.

The Total Return, or "Buy-Write," Approach

Covered writes are often referred to in the industry as "buy-writes." When you have changed your approach from picking stocks for their long-term potential to picking stocks you can specifically sell calls on, you will have crossed the bridge from being a stock picker to being a covered writer. And when you have decided to grow your overall portfolio over time through a steady stream of call premiums coupled with stock appreciation, then you will have embraced the *total return*, or *buy-write*, approach to covered writing. This is simply the generalized approach that seeks growth through the total opportunities presented by both a stock and its call options together, and that recognizes covered call writing as your primary ongoing investment strategy.

When you write covered calls on a continuous basis, you are trading some or all of a stock's uncertain potential gain in exchange for the benefit of an immediate and certain cash return in the form of a stream of revenue from the call options. In this manner, you are able to monetize in advance the potential return on a stock position during a given time period. You get to choose how long that period is and how much of the return you want to monetize through the selection of expiration month and the strike price of the call. If you sell in-the-money calls, you essentially monetize all the potential return in the stock for the period. In so doing, you are choosing to have your entire return come from the time value in the option premium you receive and none from the stock itself. By using at-the-money and out-of-the-money calls in different months, you can adjust the strategy to reach a balance between option premium and potential stock gain with which you are comfortable.

In the total return approach, you select both stocks and calls based on their attractiveness as part of a covered write. This is a departure from selecting stocks based solely on their long-term fundamentals (their basic financial status and business prospects). As a covered writer, you also want positive fundamentals, but you can loosen the requirements quite a bit in terms of price and time objectives, since the stock simply has to have a strong likelihood of being above the strike price of the call by expiration. Furthermore, the call premium has to be attractive relative to the stock price and to the call's theoretical value. (How you identify such situations will be discussed later.)

Buy-writers can identify potential investment opportunities in two ways: (1) by identifying stocks they really like and seeing whether they have options traded on them, or (2) by screening all the attractive covered writes to find those involving stocks they like. Since options are available on only a relatively small percentage of stocks, this latter method is the more efficient and can be accomplished using software programs or Internet-based services. (This process and available resources are discussed in Chapter 9.)

As a buy-write practitioner, once you have become familiar with a number of optionable stocks, chances are you will return to that group again and again for new ideas when funds are available. If, for example, you like the fundamentals on Apple Computer and establish a covered write only to have your shares called away after a month or two, you are likely to find subsequent opportunities in Apple during the following months. In fact, it is common to reestablish a position in some of the same stocks repeatedly when the share price and the option premium remain attractive.

Investors who take the total-return approach to covered writing range from quite conservative to highly aggressive. The conservative investor would select less volatile stocks and write calls that are closer to being at the money and a little farther out in time. The aggressive investor would look for stocks more likely to make big moves and would write out-of-the-money options in nearby months. Of course, there is nothing to say that you can't do some of both or vary your posture over time.

The Incremental Approach

Probably the most commonly attempted covered call writing strategy is writing calls on an existing portfolio of stocks to generate incremental income or protect gains on those holdings. This is also one of the simplest approaches, since the stocks are already in place and you only need to find an appropriate call to write. You add income while assuming zero additional risk on the downside. Like all covered writing, however, it does involve an opportunity loss on the upside, a consideration that is all too frequently ignored. The strategy typically involves writing out-of-the-money calls—to leave room for the stock to go up before the writer has to worry about being assigned—and may utilize various expiration periods.

Following are examples of circumstances that lend themselves well to incremental call writing:

- **Increasing income:** You hold a stock that you picked up at $28 and that has traded between $20 and $40 over the past eighteen months. The share price is now $30. You have finally decided that if the stock gets back up to $35, you're going to take your 25 percent gain and sell it. Once you can say that to yourself, this becomes a covered write candidate.

  —*Advantage*: It turns out that you can write a call at the 35 strike price for three months and take in $1.00 per share (less commissions). As long as you have decided you want to sell if the stock gets to $35, the income from the call is gravy. In addition, if the stock does not reach $35 in that time, you are at least $1 closer to your objective.

  —*Disadvantage:* If the stock goes to $35 in one month instead of three months, you will be faced with a dilemma. The price of the call may then be more than you sold it for. So, if you sell the stock and close the call at that time, you might have to take a loss on the option position. You can do nothing and wait, but then the stock may trade back down below $35 again by expiration. If it does, you keep the option premium and can write another call, but you may have missed the opportunity to get $35 on the stock.

▪ **Establishing a target price:** You have a stock that tends to trade in a range, and it is currently near the top of that range. Rather than sell your shares while they are high, hoping to re-purchase them later, at the bottom of the trading range, you might find a call option with a strike above the current share price and take that premium in as income. Say that, as above, the trading range is $20 to $40 and that the stock price is now $38. You might sell a call with a 40 strike. If the stock pulls back, you get to keep the premium. If it breaks out of its range on the upside and exceeds $40, you could let it get called away or roll the option out and up to a higher strike price.

—*Advantage:* If you do not want to try to outguess the stock's trading pattern, writing a call at the high end of the trading range provides additional income on the stock and will re-sult in a sale only if the shares trade above where they are currently—$40, in the above example. If assigned, you will have sold the stock at the top of its recent range and added to your proceeds whatever you received for the call.

—*Disadvantage:* If the stock breaks out above $40 and runs to, say, $45, you would not participate in that move. While you can roll up or out in that situation, you may have to increase your cost to do so.

▪ **Reducing volatility:** You hold a substantial number of stocks on which there are listed options and would like to reduce the volatility of your portfolio by bringing in some income. Or you may simply feel that the market will remain relatively flat for some time because of the overall economic climate.

—*Advantage:* You can handpick the stocks you want to write options on, and you can vary the time periods if you like. (An alternative is writing index options against the entire portfolio, but that would require substantial margin.) You can also vary the number of options you write on individual stocks. Writing fewer options leaves more upside potential and gives you more flexibility to roll up for a credit if one or more of the stocks rises.

—*Disadvantage:* If your portfolio begins to rise, you may have positions called away, forcing you to make reinvestment decisions and face potential tax consequences.

▪ **Generating current income from a long-term holding:** You own a stock with a very long investment horizon, but you believe it will only be an average performer over the next few months. You may, for example, have purchased stock in a company developing a new drug or technology that is not expected to produce revenue for many months, or even years. While waiting for longer-term developments, you write calls.

—*Advantage:* You are able to generate current income while waiting for the position to appreciate.

—*Disadvantage:* You may write a call and then see the stock rise dramatically a few days later when a major announcement is made. Then you may regret having capped the upside with a call option. While you could roll the option up or out, the process may repeat itself as additional announcements are made. Note, however, that you will still most likely have made a net profit on your positions, even if you gave up some of the upside by writing calls.

▪ **Loss repair:** One of your stocks has declined sharply, and you'd like to recoup part of that loss quickly. Accordingly, you write an out-of-the-money call option on it.

—*Advantage:* If an immediate recovery is unlikely or further decline is possible, writing calls may help you recover the loss over time. And when a stock drops rapidly, the volatility frequently rises, meaning that call premiums expand relative to the stock price and are therefore more attractive to a covered writer.

—*Disadvantage:* Writing calls on a stock that has declined limits your recovery potential during the term of the option. If the stock rebounds quickly, you might have been better off simply holding on.

Although relatively easy to implement, the incremental income approach to covered writing can be problematic and may disillusion those who try it. The crux of the matter is that additional income generated by selling calls on existing stocks can look like "free" money. Write an out-of-the-money call on a stock position every three months, and it's almost like getting a quarterly dividend on the stock (or enlarging an existing one). Now you have a stock portfolio you like for the long term, and you've increased its return by a few more percentage points annually. What could be wrong with that picture?

What is wrong is the idea that option income is "free" money. The trade-off in lost upside potential too often gets lost in the logic. At some point, one or more of the stocks will exceed the option strike price at or before expiration. The stockholder will then have to buy back the call before it expires (perhaps at a loss), or have the stock called away, or need to roll the position. The loss on the option or the opportunity loss on the stock could easily be enough to wipe out months of the extra income that was previously generated. In addition, the assignment could create an unexpected tax liability on the stock if there is a capital gain. The incremental approach therefore makes sense *only* for situations where you are truly willing to sell the stock at the strike price of the calls you write or are prepared to take a loss on the option to prevent that from happening.

The lure of free money was behind the creation of several mutual funds in the 1980s. The idea was that the fund managers would create a portfolio of quality stocks with reasonably high dividends, such as utilities, and then write call options against them to further enhance the income. These "option income" funds were positioned as hybrids between fixed-yield and regular stock funds, and they were targeted at conservative investors looking for an attractive yield plus the opportunity for some additional growth.

Most of these funds eventually closed—not because they lost money, but because they failed to deliver the promised attractive yield with upside growth potential. The yield was there, but the growth lagged that of the general market during the period. The funds also had problems with executions. Managers tried to write far out-of-the-money options on the premise that these would leave plenty of upside and that, however small the premiums earned, they would still enhance returns. But high-dividend stocks (frequently utilities) tend to be less volatile. They therefore have lower option premiums and tend not to have strike prices much higher than where the stock currently trades. So the funds gave up significant upside appreciation for a meager amount of additional yield.

This is not to say that writing incremental calls on an existing portfolio is ineffective. It can be quite effective. It's just important to manage one's expectations about the benefits and consequences of such a strategy.

Hedging Individual Stocks

When you write a call against a stock position, you are reducing the downside risk of the stock position by the amount of premium you take in. If you are writing out-of-the-money calls for incremental income, you are generally taking in a relatively small amount of money—perhaps a percentage point or two of the value of your portfolio. This may represent adequate incremental income, but it doesn't provide protection against a decline of, say, 10 to 20 percent. If you are concerned about such downside risk, or if you simply want to protect some of the gains in a stock position, you can write calls for that purpose as well. Instead of writing out-of-the-money calls, though, you would look for ones that are at or in the money.

Say you hold Microsoft shares and you'd prefer not to sell them, but you fear the stock could drop in the next couple of months and want to hedge against that decline, if possible. One way to do this is to purchase put options, which would guarantee your ability to sell the stock at a specific price. This strategy will preserve your upside and give you total protection on the downside, but it will cost you the price of the put. An alternative way to hedge your position is by writing covered calls. In doing so, you are hedged only up to the amount of premium you receive from the call, but you are taking in money rather than spending it on a put.

Example:
Microsoft (MSFT) = $58
Current date is February
MSFT Mar 55 call = 4.20
MSFT Apr 55 call = 5.60
MSFT Apr 60 call = 2.60
MSFT Jul 60 call = 4.70

Any of the calls listed above will hedge your Microsoft stock to some degree against a possible decline in the next month or so. Which one you choose depends on how much of your position you want to hedge and over what time period. The Mar 55 call, for example, hedges the stock price down to $53.80 (current price minus the premium). The April call provides only about 25 percent more premium protection. That may not be worth capping your upside for another month. If you want a little hedge but still want to leave room on the upside, you could sell the March or April 60 calls. If you are concerned about the possibility of a steep drop and are willing to give away your upside entirely for a month, then you could sell an in-the-money call, such as a March 50 or 45.

Reducing Risk in Small Portfolios

In professionally managed equity portfolios, the most commonly used method of reducing overall risk is diversification. In fact, the only other method (outside of hedging with derivatives) is to hold a portion of the portfolio in cash, which may defeat the purpose of having an equity portfolio in the first place. Meaningful risk reduction through diversification generally means you need to have at least 20 to 30 different positions (mutual funds frequently strive for well over 100). So how do individuals with $150,000 portfolios—much less ones worth $50,000—achieve meaningful diversification? They don't, pure and simple.

For such portfolios, and even those quite a bit larger, covered call writing can substitute for diversification as a valid means of reducing the overall risk. In addition, option premiums taken in can be used to buy more stocks. This enables the investor to broaden the stock base in the portfolio as well as to achieve dollar cost averaging as option premiums come in over time.

Writing Calls on "Hot" Stocks

If you like to "follow the action" and play hot (highly active) issues, you probably have experienced some serious bumps and bruises in your day. Frequently, the action involves a stock that has listed options, giving you an alternative way to participate without as much risk.

The action may be hot for a variety of reasons—possible merger or acquisition, large potential deal pending, earnings speculation, stock split, new product announcement, or rumors of all kinds. If you've participated in these types of situations, you know that some work out, but many do not. Most become roller-coaster rides regardless of how they ultimately turn out. Generally, there is speculation about a substantial move on the stock one way or the other. If an up move is what you're looking for, a covered write might be well worth considering. You may not have as much ultimate upside potential as if you simply owned the underlying stock, but you may be able to get a very attractive potential return with much less risk, and you will have a greater likelihood of making at least some profit than the stock buyer. Sometimes, when the speculation continues for months with no big move, your comrades who bought the stock are suffering from anxiety while you're pulling in option premiums.

Consider the case of InterMune (ITMN). The company develops and commercializes products for the treatment of serious pulmonary and infectious diseases and cancer. The stock, which had been as high as $52 in the preceding year, hit a low of around $16 in July 2002 before moving up to $20 in the next few weeks. In early August, call volumes and premiums began to rise precipitously. Rumors were circulating that the company would announce the results before Labor Day of clinical trials on a potentially lucrative new drug in testing. The company's future could be so profoundly affected by the results of the clinical trials that the stock might either skyrocket or collapse, depending on whether they were favorable or unfavorable.

We looked at the stock when it was trading between $20 and $21 and decided that the premiums in the September call options made covered writes very attractive. We bought the stock at $20.80 and, at the same time, were able to get the almost-unheard-of price of 4.00 for the September 22.5 call (with one month to go before expiration!). That gave us a net cost of $16.80 for the covered write, enabling us to profit even if the stock *dropped* by 10 to 15 percent. For the next two weeks, the stock traded up to $22 and back to $18. Then, on August 28, the announcement came. It was good news, but not the blockbuster some had expected. By the end of the day, the stock was at

$22.66, and the Sep 22.5 call was priced at 2.25. If the position was closed on those prices, the comparison of covered write to stock purchase for the period would look like this (excluding commissions):

Covered Write versus Stock Purchase for ITMN

Stock Purchase		Covered Write (Selling Sep 22.5 Call)
Cost	$20.80	$20.80
Gain	$1.86	$1.86 (stock)
		+ $1.75 (call)
		$3.61 (Total)
Raw % gain	8.9%	17.4%

Additionally, anyone who purchased the Sep 22.5 call at 4.00 obviously lost nearly half of their investment if they closed it on the day of the announcement.

Tax Deferral Strategies

Covered writing cannot eliminate a tax responsibility, but it can help you postpone one. Say you have owned a stock for many years and have a sizable capital gain on it. You wish to sell it, but it is late in the year, and you would like to postpone your capital gains liability for another whole year. In the meantime, however, you are afraid the stock may retreat from its current price. Writing an in-the-money call option with an expiration in the next calendar year could provide you with the downside protection you need until after year end. You don't want to go very far in the money with the call, however, because you do not want to risk having an early assignment that could negate your plan entirely.

Bear in mind that tax rules prohibit this practice until your stock position has exceeded the requirement to qualify as long term. If your position is still short term, then writing an in-the-money call could eliminate your existing holding period and restart the clock when the call is closed. You can, however, write an out-of-the-money call without incurring this restriction, although this may not provide you with as much downside protection. (The tax rules for options are explained in Chapter 7.)

The Benefits of Covered Writing 5

The first rule is not to lose. The second rule is not to forget the first rule.

WARREN BUFFETT

AMERICA'S LOVE AFFAIR WITH STOCK INVESTING IS FIRMLY grounded. With all its flaws, uncertainties, and risks, the stock market is still a highly liquid form of investment that has provided decades of good returns. The other major classes of investments—government securities, real estate, bank products, commodities, bonds, precious metals, collectibles, and so on—offer diversification opportunities, but the standout favorite for long-term growth is stock. The mainstream approach to stock investing is to buy a set of diversified quality stocks and hold them for the long term. That sounds good until you try to determine exactly what constitutes a "quality" stock and what time period qualifies as "long term." Covered call writing has numerous advantages over this buy-and-hold style of stock investing. Some of these advantages are concrete and quantifiable. Others are intangible and cannot be quantified but are equally important to an investor in the long run. Chapter 6 examines the intangibles. This chapter looks at the most easily quantifiable benefits: returns.

THE RATIONALE BEHIND COVERED WRITING

Except for commissions, options are essentially a zero-sum game. Theoretically, if call options were *perfectly valued,* they would provide an expected return of zero to buyers over a long period of time or over a large number of stocks. If such were the case, one would expect a covered option writer, over a long period of time, also to realize a zero incremental return, or a return equal to that of a buy-and-hold stock buyer (except for the difference in transaction costs and possibly taxes). But, still speaking theoretically, if it were possible to construct a portfolio of stocks with covered options that were, in reality, overvalued, the covered writer could expect to exceed the returns from a straight buy-and-hold portfolio of the same stocks over time. Recent analysis of more than a decade of data, which is discussed in detail later in this chapter, gives concrete support to this theory.

While this theory raises intriguing academic prospects for the long-term application of the strategy, it does little to help an investor determine what covered writing might do in his or her individual portfolio. In reality, of course, there are numerous variables and variations on implementation which will dramatically affect the results of individual portfolios, regardless of size. The discussion below is intended to provide both individual investors and professional money managers with a perspective on these variables that will help them formulate a realistic expectation of what they can achieve with covered call writing.

REALISTIC EXPECTATIONS

For individuals as well as professionals, actual returns are arguably less important than how well actual returns meet expectations. It doesn't matter whether the expectations are scientifically determined or are just rough ideas about what the strategy should return. They are still critical, regardless of whether they were realistic to begin with or not. Unfortunately, you won't receive much of a discussion of potential covered writing returns from the brokerage industry. Typical of the industry's approach is the following statement:

In general, covered writing will tend to provide a greater return than the overall market averages during bear market periods, flat periods, and even slightly up periods. Covered writing will tend to yield lower total returns than the market averages during strongly up periods. Bear in mind, of course, that your actual results could vary considerably from this generalized benchmark depending on your degree of diversification and the way you implement the strategy.

This chapter endeavors to quantify a little better than that the results you might expect in various circumstances. Still, with all the variables involved and with so many different ways to implement the strategy, creating realistic expectations is challenging, to say the least. The approach taken, therefore, will be to provide you with an understanding of what determines and affects returns, so that you are in a better position to develop a reasonable expectation based on the way you implement the strategy.

CALL WRITING AND STOCK RETURNS

Since covered call writing is an equity-related strategy, it is advisable to view the return expectations of any single position in the context of the underlying stock, and the expectations of the strategy over time in the context of the overall equity market environment. Chapter 3 described how the risk/reward for a covered write compared with that of owning stock by itself during the same period. Figure 3-2 showed that if the price of the stock declines, or even remains flat by expiration, the premiums received will always cause the covered write to outperform owning the stock (as long as there is time value in the option when you sell it). If the stock goes up substantially by expiration, the covered write will underperform. But by how much? And what does *substantially* mean here?

To quantify this a little better, you can begin by determining the crossover price between the covered write and the stock alone. That is the price of the stock at expiration above which the stock returns more and below which the covered write returns more for the period. Figure 5-1, which graphs the same covered write as figure 3-2, illustrates. The table in figure 5-2 quantifies the differences pictured by

Figure 5-1   Difference in Return for Covered Write versus Long Stock

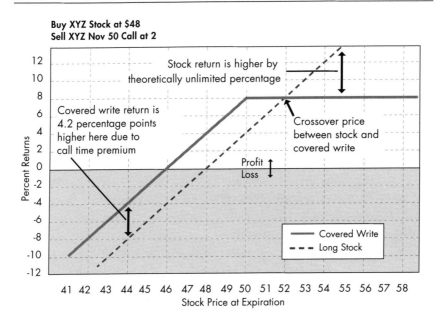

comparing the returns for expiration prices from 10 points below to 10 points above the current price of XYZ stock.

Note that the returns from covered writing exceed those of the stock by a maximum of 4.2 percentage points. Where does that number come from? It is the return unchanged discussed in Chapter 3, or the incremental return from the time value of the option. The most a return from covered writing can ever exceed the return on the underlying stock alone is the increment that comes from the time premium in the option. When you write an out-of-the-money call, the entire premium you receive consists of time value. So, if you want to get a quick sense of how much better a covered write can do than simply owning the underlying stock, just divide the time value of the option by the price you would pay for the stock.

Above the crossover price, the return on the stock can exceed the return on the covered write by a theoretically unlimited amount. Hence, at a price of $58 in this example, the stock returns 20.8 percent for the period, compared with 8.3 percent for the covered write.

This discussion shows where the statement, quoted above, about

Figure 5-2   Difference in Percentage Returns for Stock versus Covered Write
(Using hypothetical example from figure 5-1)

Stock Price	Stock Return %	CW Return %	Stock Price	Stock Return %	CW Return %
38	-20.8%	-16.7%	49	+2.1%	+6.3%
39	-18.8%	-14.6%	50	+4.2%	+8.3%
40	-16.7%	-12.5%	51	+6.3%	+8.3%
41	-14.6%	-10.4%	52	**+8.3%**	**+8.3%**
42	-12.5%	-8.3%	53	+10.4%	+8.3%
43	-10.4%	-6.3%	54	+12.5%	+8.3%
44	-8.3%	-4.2%	55	+14.6%	+8.3%
45	-6.3%	-2.1%	56	+16.7%	+8.3%
46	-4.2%	0	57	+18.8%	+8.3%
47	-2.1%	+2.1%	58	+20.8%	+8.3%
48	0	**+4.2 %**			

Crossover Price

Return Unchanged

the strategy's returns in different environments comes from: "Covered writing will tend to provide a greater return than the overall market averages during bear market periods, flat periods, and even slightly up periods"—that is, covered writing outperforms for all prices up to the crossover price. "Covered writing will tend to yield lower total returns than the market averages during strongly up periods"—above the crossover price, the stock alone does better by an amount that increases with the price of the stock. Thus, the key to how much covered writing might outperform the underlying stock is how much time premium you get when you write, and the key to how much covered writing might underperform the stock is the level of the strike price you are writing. If your writing protocol is fairly consistent—for example, if you always write slightly out-of-the-money 60-day calls—then you will have a good sense of the crossover point on the positions you initiate and can quickly compute in your head rough estimates of potential returns under different scenarios.

Figuring the covered write return for a given stock price is the easy part. The hard part is determining a likely scenario for the stock itself. You can use technical analysis (price charts) to reckon a stock's reasonable price range in the short term, or you can just use your judgment. Either way, the best anyone can reasonably do is come up with a range of possible prices. That said, it is possible to calculate the mathematical probability of a stock reaching a strike price by using its historical volatility (free calculators that enable you to do this yourself are available at websites discussed in Chapter 9). Say that XYZ stock in the example above has a historical volatility of 40 percent. Assuming that the call has fifty days until expiration, that means the *statistical* likelihood of XYZ trading above the strike price is 39 percent, and that of its trading above the break-even price is 61 percent.

MAJOR FACTORS AFFECTING CALL WRITING RETURNS

Your returns from covered writing will clearly depend on how you implement the strategy—your choice of stock, strike price, expiration—as well as on other external factors, such as interest rates and transaction costs.

Stock Selection

In picking stocks for a covered writing portfolio, you will find that you will use a somewhat different set of criteria from that employed to select stocks for outright purchase. As you hone your selection skills and fine-tune your criteria for this task, your returns are likely to improve. Also important is the degree of diversification of your portfolio: The more diversified, the more your returns will correlate with overall market conditions. The less diversified, the greater the impact of stock selection.

Your consistency in implementing your strategy can also have a substantial impact on your returns. If you elect not to write calls at certain times, or do not reinvest your capital after assignments, you cannot expect your results to track as closely to the underlying stock or to your overall benchmark as you might hope. That doesn't mean you will necessarily do worse. It just means that your results will not be as predictable relative to your expectations.

Strike Price

The strike price with the greatest amount of time value is always the one closest to the current price of the stock. Consequently, the farther away the strike price is from the current stock price, the lower the static return (return unchanged) for the position. The table in figure 5-3 illustrates this point with Merrill Lynch (MER) calls, priced with just under two months until September '02 expiration.

Remember that this is not the only factor you should consider when deciding which strike to write. Lower strike prices will provide greater downside protection, while higher strike prices offer greater potential gains from the stock. You should, however, understand how these tradeoffs affect your static return.

You can see from the table that the difference between writing the Sep 35 call and the Sep 40 call is 5.4 percentage points. Remember that this is only a two-month return. On an annualized basis, the difference between writing the near-the-money call and the next higher strike price is more than 30 percentage points in return. Of course, this is the static return and therefore ignores appreciation in the stock, but it gives you a perspective on how much return from option premium

Figure 5-3 Percent Return from Different Strike Prices (Using MER September 2002 calls, with MER at $34.20 and 58 days until expiration)

Strike Price	Premium (Bid Price)	Time Value	% Return from Time Value (Return Unchanged)
20	14.20	0	0%
22.5	11.90	0.20	0.6%
25	9.70	0.50	1.5%
27.5	7.70	1.00	2.9%
30	5.90	1.70	5.0%
32.5	4.30	2.60	7.6%
35	**3.00**	**3.00**	**8.8%**
37.5	1.90	1.90	5.6%
40	1.15	1.15	3.4%
42.5	0.60	0.60	1.8%
45	0.30	0.30	0.9%
47.5	0.10	0.10	0.3%

Static returns drop as you select a strike price farther away from the current price of the stock.

Source: PowerOptionsPlus

you give up when you write a higher strike price in the hope that the stock will move up. The higher you go in strike price, the greater the *potential* return from a covered write, but the lower the contribution from option premium and the more uncertain the overall return.

Expiration

The selection of expiration month will also affect the expected returns of your covered writing program, because options do not lose time value (decay) at the same rate throughout their life. The differing rate of decay is important and can have a significant effect on the returns from the strategy. It is also why we have emphasized in this book the fact that covered writing is a short-term strategy.

You might expect that if you could receive a premium of X by writing an out-of-the-money call option with one month till expiration, you would get a premium of 2X for writing the same strike price two months out. (Remember, the entire premium in an out-of-the-money call is time value.) In reality, you should expect to get somewhat less than 2X (all other things being equal). The reason is that option premiums do not decay linearly with time. Instead, they decay more slowly in the early months and more rapidly as they approach expiration. More precisely, the Black-Scholes formula predicts that the time value of an option will decay as the *square root* of time remaining until expiration. Figure 5-4 represents this relationship graphically.

Thus a call with four months until expiration will not have four times as much premium as one with a similar strike price and one month to go. Instead, it will have approximately twice as much premium, since $\sqrt{4} = 2$. This means that the rate of decay in the time value of an option is (theoretically) fastest in the last month before expiration, slowing with each successive month farther from that date. Therefore, while you take in more total premium from a more distant option, you take in *proportionately less* for the extra time and will lower your annualized return potential from the position. Conversely, the closer the option is to its expiration, the more time value *per day* the writer will receive. (This is illustrated in the "premium per day" column of the table in figure 5-5, which lists actual premiums for Merrill Lynch calls.)

Figure 5-4 Graph of Time Value Decay in an Option

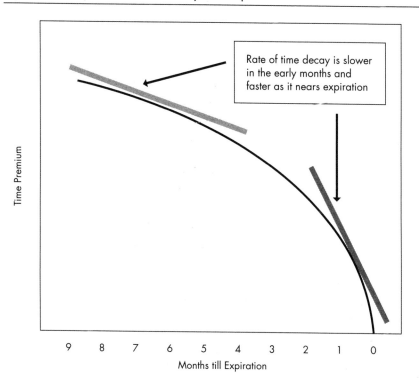

Greater time premium per day on the same initial investment translates into higher potential returns. Therefore, if you are an option writer, you can achieve better annualized returns (all other things being equal) by writing options closer to expiration than by writing the same strike prices farther out. The difference can be considerable.

Bear in mind that the square root relationship is theoretical. Thus, it should be used as a guide and not held as a given. The table in figure 5-5 shows the differing time values and returns for Merrill Lynch call options with the same strike price but different expirations. The strike used is 35, because it is out-of-the-money and the entire premium will therefore be time value. The returns are annualized for comparison purposes, since the time periods involved are all different.

From the above analysis, you might conclude that it is always best to write the closest option available, since it will provide more time value per day and accordingly generate higher potential returns. The pri-

Figure 5-5 Percent Return from Different Expiration Months (Using MER calls with stock at $34.20)

Expiration Month	Premium (Bid Price)	Days Left	Premium Per Day	% Return Unchanged (Annualized)
Aug 35 call	1.80	23	0.078	83.5%
Sep 35 call	3.00	58	0.052	55.2%
Oct 35 call	3.50	86	0.041	43.4%
Jan 35 ('03) call	4.40	177	0.025	26.5%
Jan 35 ('04) LEAP	7.00	541	0.013	13.8%

Source: PowerOptionsPlus

> Static returns can be much greater from options that are closer to expiration.

mary counter-argument is that the near-month call has the least amount of *absolute* premium and therefore offers the least amount of downside protection, should the stock decline. You do take in more total premium by using a more distant expiration month. However, you don't necessarily gain much in near-term protection unless the stock falls considerably during the first month. Using the Merrill Lynch example again, the table in figure 5-6 shows how much protection would be provided by the various expiration months available in scenarios in which the stock drops in the first month to $32, $30, and $25.

The table shows that which expiration provides the most protection depends on how much the stock actually drops. In general, for better overall returns from covered writing, you will want to write a relatively close option most of the time. But if you want protection from the possibility of a significant drop in price, a more distant call may be warranted.

Volatility

In a way, your stock selection takes volatility into account, but its effect on option premiums can be isolated to help you gauge the potential returns from stocks with different volatilities. This is illustrated in the table in figure 5-7, which lists the theoretical premiums of at-the-money calls on a hypothetical stock using different volatilities. Figure 5-8 shows a typical range of volatilities through a

Figure 5-6   Downside Protection from Different Expiration Months

Expiration Month	Option Price When Sold	Option Price after One Month	Protection Provided
MER drops to $32			
Aug 35 call	1.80	0	1.80
Sep 35 call	3.00	1.36	1.64
Oct 35 call	3.50	2.15	1.35
Jan 35 ('03) call	4.40	4.10	0.30
MER drops to $30			
Aug 35 call	1.80	0	1.80
Sep 35 call	3.00	0.75	2.25
Oct 35 call	3.50	1.40	2.10
Jan 35 ('03) call	4.40	3.10	1.30
MER drops to $25			
Aug 35 call	1.80	0	1.80
Sep 35 call	3.00	0.10	2.90
Oct 35 call	3.50	0.35	3.15
Jan 35 ('03) call	4.40	1.38	3.02

Source: CBOE option calculator

> The option that theoretically provides the most downside protection depends on how much the stock actually drops.

sampling of optionable stocks. Volatility is typically calculated as a standard deviation of the daily price movements in a stock over a specific time period, which is annualized and expressed as a percent. It may be interpreted as indicating the probability (derived from the definition of standard deviation) that the stock will trade within a certain range within a certain period. For instance, a volatility of 40 percent means that during the period for which it was calculated (typically 20, 50, or 100 days), two-thirds of the time, the stock's price was within 40 percent up or down from its mean. By itself, this statistic is of little use to most investors. But as a comparative measure, either to other stocks or to other time periods for the same stock, it can be very useful in deciding whether a covered write on that stock offers an attractive risk/reward situation.

Many stocks with listed options have volatilities well in excess of 100 percent. One should not, however, jump to the conclusion

Figure 5-7   Percent Returns at Different Volatility Levels (Stock Price = $30, Strike Price = 30, Days to Expiration = 46, Interest Rate = 5%)

Volatility*	Option Bid (Time Value)	Return Unchanged† (Not Annualized)
0.10	0.60	2.0%
0.20	1.10	3.8%
0.30	**1.55**	**5.4%**
0.40	2.00	7.1%
0.50	2.50	9.1%
0.60	**3.00**	**11.1%**
0.70	3.45	13.0%
0.80	3.95	15.2%
0.90	4.40	17.2%
1.00	4.90	19.5%

Twice the volatility means twice the potential return (all else being equal)

*Calculated using a 100-day period. †Calculated using the net debit method.
Source: McMillan Analysis Corp.

that writing calls on the most volatile stocks will necessarily provide the highest returns. While their premiums, and thus the potential returns, are indeed greater, the downside risk is proportionately greater as well. The way to achieve higher expected returns over time is not by writing calls on stocks with high volatility per se, but by writing calls on stocks where the *implied* volatility (that forecast by the price of the call option) is greater than the actual volatility will be for the period of the option. (Implied volatility and the valuation of options are discussed in detail in Chapter 8.)

Figure 5-8   Sample Volatilities for Stocks in the Dow Jones Industrial Average (100-day volatility as of 9/1/2002)

Highest Volatility Dow Stocks			Lowest Volatility Dow Stocks		
Symbol	Name	Volatility	Symbol	Name	Volatility
INTC	Intel	0.73	DD	DuPont	0.34
JPM	JP Morgan Chase	0.66	CAT	Caterpillar	0.34
C	Citigroup	0.58	MCD	McDonalds	0.32
HD	Home Depot	0.52	KO	Coca-Cola	0.30
JNJ	Johnson & Johnson	0.43	PG	Procter & Gamble	0.28

Source: McMillan Analysis Corp.

Interest Rates

Since option premiums are affected by interest rates, returns from covered writing will be as well. It takes a substantial move in rates, however, to affect premiums. (LEAPS options of one or more years in duration are much more sensitive.) Figure 5-9 shows the effect of different interest rates on premiums and returns for a hypothetical two-month option.

Transaction Costs

Since covered writing involves buying and selling both stocks and options on an ongoing basis, transaction costs can have a material impact on the strategy's returns. Before the introduction of discount commissions and online brokerage services, the costs for retail customers were high enough to eat away a major portion of the expected returns from any strategy that involved more than a few transactions a year. In fact, covered option writing is not recommended for anyone who pays full-service commissions. Discount commissions are markedly lower and have only a minor impact on returns, but they still do have *some* impact, particularly if you have a small account.

A relatively new type of account has emerged at full-service firms in the past few years that charges a fixed fee—typically a per-

Figure 5-9   Effect of Interest Rates on Option Returns (Stock Price = $30, Strike Price = 30, Days to Expiration = 57, Volatility = 0.30)

Interest Rate	Premium	Return Unchanged (Not Annualized)
2.0%	1.46	4.9%
3.0%	1.49	5.0%
4.0%	1.51	5.0%
5.0%	1.53	5.1%
6.0%	1.56	5.2%
7.0%	1.58	5.3%
8.0%	1.60	5.3%
9.0%	1.63	5.4%
10.0%	1.65	5.5%

> Interest rates have a negligible effect on returns of short-term options unless they move dramatically

Source: PowerOptionsPlus

centage of your total assets—each quarter and then allows you a substantial number of trades with no commissions. The largest brokerage firms all have versions of this type of account, among them *Morgan Stanley Choice*SM, *Merrill Lynch Unlimited Advantage*SM, and *Smith Barney AssetOne*®. Fees tend to run about 1 to 2 percent of assets a year, or even less, depending on the size of your account. Minimum account fees of around $1,000 to $1,500 a year typically apply, and a balance of $50,000 is generally required to start. Since a 1 to 2 percent fee amounts to what you could pay in standard full-service commissions on just a few transactions, these fixed-fee accounts are definitely the way to go if you engage in covered writing with a full-service firm. For active accounts, you may even find that fixed fees compare quite favorably with the commissions you would incur at a discount broker.

To illustrate the effect of transaction costs on covered writing returns, figure 5-10 compares the returns for three trades of different volumes using a typical discount brokerage commission rate and a typical full-service commission rate with no discount. (These figures come from a prominent discount broker and a full-service brokerage firm.)

Figure 5-10   Effect of Transaction Costs on Covered Writing Returns
(Stock Price = $30, Strike = 30, Days to Expiration = 57, call = 2)

Position Size	Position Value	Return Unchanged (Not Annualized)		Return after Commissions	
		Dollars	Percent	Discount	Full-Service
100 shares & 1 option	$3,000	$200	6.7%	4.4%	0%
500 shares & 5 options	$15,000	$1,000	6.7%	6.2%	2.1%
1000 shares & 10 options	$30,000	$2,000	6.7%	6.4%	2.8%

Note: Stock is assumed to be sold at expiration.

Even discount commissions will have an impact in very small accounts

Full-service commissions can wipe out almost all the profits from the strategy

COVERED WRITES COMPARED WITH STOCKS OVER TIME

Professional investment managers have long known covered call writing to be a valuable technique for generating income and lowering the risks of stock portfolios. But, for the most part, they have implemented the strategy on only a few select positions, if at all. In part, this was because the prevailing expectation was that writing calls on their stock positions would lower their portfolios' long-term returns. Only recently has the professional investment community put this proposition to the test of actual data. Following are two analyses of covered write performance over a period exceeding 10 years, each using a mechanically implemented program. This is applied, in the first case, to the S&P 500 stocks as a group and, in the second, to a number of individual stocks.

The BuyWrite Index (BXM)

In May 2002, the Chicago Board Options Exchange, or CBOE, the nation's largest option exchange, created an index to track a basic covered writing strategy. The resulting *CBOE BuyWrite Monthly Index*[SM] *(BXM)* simulates the performance of a strategy consisting of writing the one-month call option at the nearest out-of-the money strike price on the Standard & Poor's 500 stock index every month. As each option expires, the net gain or loss is registered, and the next month's option is written. Like most other major market indexes, the BXM is designed to emulate a passive (unmanaged) return against which portfolio managers can gauge their performance on actively managed accounts. (For more information on the details of the BXM, visit the BXM microsite at www.CBOE.com.)

Although only recently introduced, the BXM has been calculated back to June 1988, when S&P began tracking the dividends on the S&P 500 Index. So the returns of the S&P 500 Index can be compared with those of a basic covered writing program (as represented by the BXM) over more than a decade. The results have created a stir among professional investment managers who spend their lives searching for ways to produce competitive returns with less risk. Figure 5-11 shows the comparison by calendar year.

Figure 5-11   Performance of the BXM versus the S&P 500

	Percent Returns by Calendar Year					
	89	90*	91	92*	93*	94*
BXM	25.0	4.0	24.4	11.5	14.1	4.5
S&P	31.7	-3.1	30.5	7.6	10.1	1.3

	Percent Returns by Calendar Year					
	95	96	97	98	99*	00*	01*
BXM	21.0	15.5	26.6	18.9	21.2	7.4	-10.9
S&P	37.6	23.0	33.4	28.6	21.1	-9.1	-11.1

> *The BXM returns were better in 7 of 13 calendar years

Total Period Return (13.58 years)
BXM   13.88%
S&P   14.07%

> The BXM returns came within 0.2 percentage points of the S&P 500 returns, averaged over the entire 13.5 years

Standard Deviation of Monthly Returns
BXM   2.67
S&P   4.10

> Calculated monthly, the BXM returns showed about two-thirds as much volatility as the S&P 500's

Source: Chicago Board Option Exchange

Additional points worth noting:

- The BXM outperformed when the S&P 500 returned 21 percent or less and underperformed when the S&P returned more than 23 percent. This is generally what covered writing is expected to do but should *not* be taken to represent a specific crossover point between the two strategies.
- In 2001, the S&P 500 returned -11.1 percent and the BXM -10.9 percent. In 2000, however, when the S&P 500 returned -9.1 percent, the BXM turned in a surprising +7.4 percent return. This illustrates how differently the covered writing portfolio can perform in years when the underlying index has similar returns.

Bear in mind that these results provide a very broad benchmark of what a basic mechanical covered writing program can do compared with the buy-and-hold approach. Your portfolio is unlikely to be anywhere near as diverse as the S&P 500. Your stocks may thus perform quite differently and may have much different volatilities. (The next section looks at how much a similar program applied to individual stocks would have returned during the same period of time.) Also, the BXM assumes a mechanically implemented program using one-month at-the-money calls only, without any rolling. And it doesn't take into account transaction costs or taxes. Nevertheless, the BXM clearly demonstrates that although the returns from covered writing may be lower than those stocks that are *capable* of producing during a given period, they are commensurate with the returns stocks *actually* generate over the long term—with a substantial reduction in volatility. Thus, it provides an important affirmation of the long-term validity of covered writing.

Real-World Results for Twenty Stocks

During the summer of 2002, the authors undertook an independent study to compare the long-term returns of a basic covered writing program applied to individual stocks with those generated by buying and holding the same stocks. This entailed building a model to simulate a covered writing program in individual stocks that was similar to the BXM's model so that the BXM could act as a benchmark for the results. For this purpose, actual price histories, going back as far as June 1988, were compiled for a sample of individual stocks and their call options.

Collecting the data was highly problematic. Daily price histories for stocks are readily available, but no one we contacted outside the CBOE had sufficient historical data on the prices of call options in electronic form, and the CBOE has so much data that the exchange said it would take months to extract what was needed from its computer archives. So, in an example of electronic-age irony, options data for the study had to be gathered manually from the *Wall Street Journal*'s microfiche records. Because the *WSJ* does not report on all options, and because of mergers and other corporate changes that have occurred during the period covered, the study includes data on nine stocks for the entire period (June 1, 1988, to December 31, 2001) and on eleven others for at least five years of the period. Although the stocks included are among the most actively traded and provide a reasonable cross section of companies, they should not be taken as a representative sample of the market as a whole, since eight of the twenty are technology related. All told, more than 2,500 expiration months in twenty stocks are included in the database.

The study used the same basic methodology as the BXM, simulating a strategy of writing one-month call options at the nearest out-of-the-money strike price. If the underlying stock was above the strike at option expiration, the model assumed it was called away and repurchased on the following Monday. If not, another out-of-the-money call was written for the next month on the following Monday (using closing prices).

To facilitate the comparison of covered writing with a buy-and-hold strategy in each stock, the model did not allow additional money to be invested anytime during the period. Thus, in the covered writing scenario, when there was not enough money to repurchase the same number of shares following an assignment, the model bought fewer shares for the next month (although it always dealt in round lots). It also, however, purchased additional round lots when cash from option premiums was sufficient to do so. And, to be realistic, it allowed idle cash to earn money-market interest and deducted charges for commissions at rates typical of a discount or online brokerage firm. (A more detailed explanation of the methodology and a list of the assumptions is found in Appendix D.)

The study provided a great deal of insight into the long-term effects of covered writing on different stocks. The period involved was long enough to include three down years in addition to the five years with greater than 25 percent equity returns that were part of the "Internet bubble"—one of the greatest bull markets ever. However, it is important to remember that the methodology for the study was designed to facilitate historical comparisons and not to represent a suggested implementation of covered writing. In practice, for example, a covered writer would not continually reestablish covered writes in the same stock after being assigned or necessarily write a one-month call option in all cases. The table in figure 5-12 on the following page summarizes the study's results.

Highlights from the study include the following:

- As expected, the returns on individual stocks varied widely from each other and from the market overall, but the variation was less extreme for covered writing than for the buy-and-hold strategy. A buy-and-hold investor in the twenty stocks studied would have earned average annualized returns for the entire period ranging from -3 percent (ASA) to 38 percent (MSFT), while a covered writer in the same stocks would have experienced a low of 2 percent (ASA) and a high of 25 percent (MSFT).

- For the overall period, covered writing outperformed buy-and-hold as a continuous strategy for seven of the twenty stocks (even after commissions). All seven of these stocks returned less than 20 percent on an average annualized basis. This is consistent with how covered writing should compare to a buy-and-hold strategy.

- The monthly returns from covered writing exhibited lower volatility than those of the buy-and-hold strategy for every stock in the sample. This was also consistent with the performance of the BXM index.

- Certain stocks provided call writing opportunities much more frequently than others. Not all stocks have the volatility necessary to generate at least $0.50 in premium for a one-month out-of-the-money call option every month. Stocks like Intel, Microsoft, IBM, Hewlett-Packard, and Cisco almost always will, but Wal-Mart, Kodak, Toys "R" Us, and Phillips Petroleum generated sufficient premium less than half of the time during the months they were studied.

- Call options expired worthless between one-half and two-thirds of the time, even for stocks in the sample that had exceptional growth rates over the period. Interestingly, assignments occurred between 28 percent and 48 percent of the time for all twenty stocks in the study and between 35 percent and 45 percent for the majority. Even the calls on high-

Figure 5-12 Summary Table for Study of Buy/Hold versus Covered Writing
(Securities are listed in order of their buy/hold returns)

Company	Symbol	Number Months	Average Annualized Percent Return Buy/Hold	CW	Percent Write	Percent Assign	Volatility of Monthly Returns B/H	CW
Stocks included in the entire period 6/88–12/01								
Microsoft	MSFT	163	38.15%	25.42%	98%	48%	10.59	6.35
Oracle	ORCL	163	36.04%	23.67%	76%	47%	17.42	13.32
Intel	INTC	163	29.13%	16.54%	93%	40%	13.33	9.09
Sun Micro-systems	SUNW	163	26.04%	25.27%	82%	35%	19.96	13.67
Philip Morris	MO	163	14.66%	9.96%	78%	45%	8.94	6.75
Merck	MRK	163	14.63%	13.80%	79%	40%	7.92	6.10
BuyWrite Index	BXM	163	14.07%	13.88%	— —	— —	4.10	2.67
IBM	IBM	163	11.30%	4.81%	99%	40%	10.90	6.20
Disney	DIS	163	11.05%	8.07%	75%	40%	26.48	21.74
Adv. Micro Devices	AMD	163	5.29%	9.10%	66%	35%	20.90	17.38
Stocks with less than 163 months of consecutive data during 6/88–12/01								
Cisco Systems	CSCO	68	20.52%	10.20%	93%	43%	14.30	10.39
Hewlett Packard	HPQ	138	19.47%	17.83%	91%	41%	10.50	6.09
WalMart	WMT	90	16.08%	17.19%	42%	29%	7.22	6.58
McDonalds	MCD	138	11.70%	12.63%	51%	43%	7.51	6.26
Minn. Mining	MMM	90	10.54%	14.00%	78%	33%	4.53	3.73
Phillips Petroleum	P	61	10.38%	10.77%	28%	35%	6.68	5.78
Toys "R" Us	TOY	102	7.49%	9.91%	43%	34%	8.02	7.04
Federal Express	FDX	78	6.00%	7.46%	73%	35%	9.56	7.47
General Motors	GM	138	5.70%	5.20%	64%	38%	8.47	6.68
Eastman Kodak	EK	66	4.86%	2.65%	44%	48%	6.07	4.58
ASA Limited	ASA	102	-2.87%	2.10%	66%	28%	7.73	5.76

Number Months = number of consecutive months between 6/88 and 12/01 for which data was available. Average Annual-ized Percent Returns **do not** include dividends but **do** include commissions. (The BXM includes dividends but not commissions.) Percent Write = the percentage of months in which a call was written. Calls were not written if the closing price of the one-month out-of-the-money call was less than $0.50 on the Monday after an expiration or if the strike price was not available. Per-cent Assign = the percentage of one-month writes that were assigned.

Source: The Wall Street Journal and BigCharts.com.

performance stocks like Oracle and Microsoft expired worthless more than half of the time.

Results by Calendar Year

As noted above, the returns of individual stocks for both strategies varied considerably from one another and from the overall market average. That was for time periods of from five to thirteen-and-a-half years. Calendar-year returns were even more divergent.

The study included 200 separate calendar-year performances. The table in Appendix D, which lists the single-year results for all of the stocks in the study, shows that the performance can vary quite dramatically from stock to stock and from year to year. Returns ranged from -66 percent to +288 percent. Interestingly, Oracle was responsible for *both* these extremes. The covered-write returns ranged from -69 percent, for Oracle, to +311 percent, for Advanced Micro Devices.

These extremes of performance provide a solid argument for diversification, but not much else in the way of insights. The data inside the extremes, however, do reveal some telling differences between covered writing and the buy-and-hold strategy. Figure 5-13, which charts the range of returns for the 200 calendar-year periods in the study, shows that covered writing provides a greater number of returns between -25 percent and +25 percent than buy-and-hold and has fewer periods with returns at the extremes.

Overall, covered writing outperformed buy-and-hold in 95 of the 200 years, underperformed in 98, and tied in 5. Thus, the study reaffirmed that covered writing can outperform a buy-and-hold approach approximately half the time while providing lower extremes in returns.

Effects of Writing a Higher Strike Price

Since, to be consistent with the BXM model, the covered writing model in the above study looked only at writing the nearest month and nearest out-of-the-money calls, a reasonably high number of assignments were generated. It's difficult to tell how a different

Figure 5-13 Distribution of Returns in 200 Calendar-Year Periods

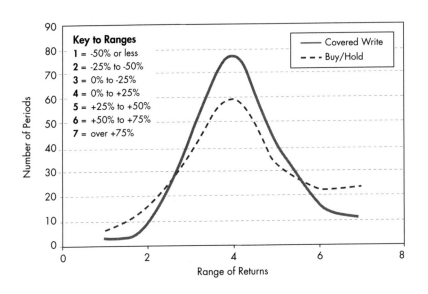

call-writing methodology might have affected those results. However, for some stocks, such as IBM and Microsoft, there was sufficient premium, even in a one-month option, to write the second-higher strike price above the current stock price—the 70 instead of the 65, for example, when the shares were trading at 62. Writing calls at a higher strike price allows more upside potential in the stock but provides less downside protection. Adjusting the model so that the second-higher strike price was written for IBM and Microsoft between 1988 and 2001 produced the results shown in figure 5-14. For Microsoft, the long-term return using the second higher strike price was greater by 4.5 percentage points than that of using the next higher strike; for IBM, the two returns were almost identical.

As discussed earlier in this chapter, returns can vary significantly with strike price and expiration month, and they can be further affected by the writer's follow-up actions, such as rolling or closing positions entirely. Thus, a covered writer can achieve results quite different from those of a benchmark like the BXM depending on how

Figure 5-14   Results When Writing the Second Higher Strike Price

Company	Symbol	Number Months	Average Annualized Percent Return Buy/Hold	CCW	Percent Write	Percent Assign	Volatility of Monthly Returns B/H	CW
*Results when writing **next** higher strike price*								
IBM	IBM	163	11.30%	4.81%	99%	40%	10.90	6.20
Microsoft	MSFT	163	38.15%	25.42%	98%	48%	10.59	6.35
*Results when writing **second** higher strike price*								
IBM	IBM	163	11.30%	4.36%	99%	29%	10.90	6.74
Microsoft	MSFT	163	38.15%	29.98%	98%	32%	10.59	7.59

> The return for IBM was almost identical and that for MFST was 4.5 percentage points higher. Both showed a reduced number of assignments.

the technique is implemented. That said, probably the most important overall insight gleaned from the individual stock study was how dramatically stock selection can affect the returns from covered writing, dwarfing the effects of strike or expiration. Stock selection is thus of greater importance in covered writing than the particulars of the methodology used.

RECAPPING BENEFITS

▪ Covered writing returns are a function of the returns of the underlying instrument. The covered write will outperform the underlying up to the crossover price (strike price plus option premium) by a fixed percentage, determined by the time value in the option. Above the crossover price, the underlying instrument will outperform the covered write by a percentage that increases with the price of the underlying and without limit.

▪ By using the historical volatility of a stock, you can derive a statistical probability of it reaching any strike price by a given expiration date.

■ The greatest amount of time value, and hence of static return, is realized by writing the call with the strike price closest to the stock's price. The farther away from the strike price in either direction, the less return you will realize from option time value.

■ The higher the strike price of the call you write, the wider the range of potential returns from the covered write.

■ The closer your calls are to expiration (all other things being equal), the greater the time premium per day you will receive, and the higher your potential annualized return will be.

■ Higher-volatility stocks have option premiums that are proportionately greater than lower-volatility stocks and will therefore offer higher *potential* returns. Writers should realize, however, that such stocks will also have proportionately greater downside risk.

■ Transaction costs can have a significant effect on returns. Covered writers need to determine for themselves whether the strategy is worthwhile at the commission rates they are paying.

■ The performance of the CBOE BuyWrite Index (BXM) between 1988 and 2001 shows that over this 13.5-year period, a basic covered writing program on the S&P 500 Index would have yielded an average annual return of 13.88 percent, compared with 14.07 percent for the S&P 500 Index itself, but with approximately one-third less deviation in monthly returns. While this performance does not take into account commissions or taxes, it demonstrates that a basic covered writing program can approximate the average annual returns for stocks alone for a broad base of stocks over a long period of time.

■ In a study of twenty individual stocks, variations in annual performance were quite dramatic. However, covered writing generated smaller extremes in annual performance and beat or matched the results of a buy-and-hold strategy using the same stocks in 103 out of 200 sample years.

Intangible Benefits 6

Take calculated risks. That is much better than being rash.

GEORGE S. PATTON

WHEN YOU CONSIDER A CHANGE IN JOB OR CAREER, DO YOU look beyond the compensation? If so, when you consider a different investment strategy, shouldn't you look beyond the potential returns? Quite a few advantages of covered writing have to do with things like investment behavior, peace of mind, and flexibility. These advantages flow in large part from the covered writer's liberation from the long-term, buy-and-hold perspective.

WHAT IS LONG TERM, ANYWAY?

The party line from investment firms has always been that since you cannot time either the market or individual stocks, you are best served by buying a diversified portfolio of stocks and holding them for the long term. But what is "long term"? When asked, most people probably proffer the somewhat arbitrary one-year period used by the Internal Revenue Service for determining whether your capital appreciation should be taxed as long- or short-term capital gains. What does the IRS know? The agency only made the distinction to encourage people to hold on to their investments longer, thus providing stability to the financial markets. There's no magic about one year—or about any other period, for that matter—as the optimum or minimal holding period for a stock.

The emphasis on a long holding period results largely from the fact that the research analysts and others who recommend stocks for a buy-and-hold strategy invariably use fundamental analysis in their selection process. Fundamental analysis steers you into a holding period of at least several quarters, because that's the typical time in which the fundamentals are expected to build themselves into the share price. (In contrast, market technicians, who follow charts and price action, will sell stock in five days or even five minutes if the situation warrants.)

You will rarely see a "sell" recommendation from a brokerage house research analyst, because it is deemed politically incorrect for them to issue one. Consequently, you are left to figure out an exit plan for yourself. Your only other choice is to have your money privately managed or toss it into a mutual fund and forget about it. Either way, you doom yourself to a market average return, if that. Covered call writing has the advantage of putting you back in control, giving you greater consistency of returns, and allowing you to tailor your holdings to your risk tolerance and to changing market conditions.

THE COVERED-WRITE SOLUTION

If you are managing at least part of your own portfolio, picking your own stocks and deciding when to buy and sell them, then you are undoubtedly wrestling with the following challenges on a regular basis:

- researching what to buy from a total exchange-listed universe of approximately 7,500 stocks (plus thousands more that are nonlisted)
- poring over fundamental research or charts and graphs to determine long-term potential

- getting emotionally involved with the companies to justify buying them
- deciding when (or at what price) to buy them
- agonizing over when to sell them
- second-guessing yourself constantly over the above decisions as markets move

And with all this, do you even know how you've performed? Of the thousands of mutual fund managers and thousands more private money managers, only a small percentage beat the overall market averages each year. And these are people who focus their entire energy on selecting and monitoring securities, have tons of information at their disposal, and frequently have staffs to assist with research. So if you can even come close to their performance, congratulate yourself and consider getting a high-paying job as a portfolio manager. If not, then you may want to consider covered writing.

Implementing a covered-write strategy liberates you from many of those stresses and strains associated with constructing a stock portfolio. Specifically, it delivers benefits such as the following:

- You no longer need to figure out whether a company has what it takes to outperform everything else in its industry and the rest of the market. Most of the time even a modestly performing stock will achieve your objectives.
- You no longer need a crystal ball through which to peer a year or two into the future. You need only have a reasonable fix on the next few months, if that.
- You can now get emotionally involved in your overall *strategy* rather than in individual stock positions.
- Your selectable universe of stocks drops from 7,500+ to about 2,300 yet still offers prominent stocks from all major industry groups.
- You can use your computer to rank candidates by potential return.
- You must review your holdings and make decisions on them each month, a discipline that prevents the dreaded investor diseases of decision paralysis and *portfolius languishus*.

- Your target selling price and holding period for any stock position will be precisely determined when you initiate your position.
- You benefit each and every day in some small way from the passage of time, regardless of whether stocks go up or down.
- You get to use other people's money (OPM) to compound your total returns.
- You can alter the risk/reward profile of your stock investments *after* you've initiated them.
- The volatility (ups and downs) of your monthly returns will be lower.
- You can achieve stock market returns with far less stress and anxiety.

THE BENEFITS IN DETAIL

You no longer need to try to figure out whether a company has what it takes to outperform. Researching companies' long-term fundamentals to determine their stocks' future potential is a noble endeavor. But we all know it is flawed. We've seen the evidence of that in spades over the past few years. Even when corporate executives are providing accurate information, research analysts at brokerage firms are hard pressed to say anything truly negative about the companies they report on. Companies are now handcuffed from saying too much about their future prospects to anyone for fear of investor lawsuits.

In the year that you own a stock and are looking for a move, there could easily be several hundred news items that affect the price one way or another. The idea that anyone can look forward a year or more and determine what the price of a company's stock should be then is more than a little suspect. So why fool yourself into thinking you can do it? The good news about covered writing is that it is much more forgiving than simply owning stocks. You don't have to be as right and you don't have to be right as often to achieve the same overall returns.

You no longer need a crystal ball through which to peer a year or two into the future. Beware! Considering stocks based on their potential over a one-month time horizon may be hazardous to your reputation. Naysayers will taunt you. People at your golf club may call you a "trader." But, hey, if that's what it takes to make money more consistently, let them call you whatever they want.

This gets right to the heart of what makes covered call writing an attractive strategy and flies directly in the face of traditional investing. Somewhere along the line, buying stocks and holding them for months or years at a time became synonymous with "investing" in many people's eyes, and buying stocks to sell them in days or weeks became synonymous with "trading"—to some, a tainted label. Lost in all of this is the idea that you buy stocks to increase your wealth, pure and simple. One of the biggest of all hypocrisies in the securities industry is the fact that while the big investment firms push their clients into long-term buy-and-hold investing, a major portion of the firms' own profits comes from their in-house trading activities. It's public knowledge. Look at their income statements. When you engage in covered writing on an ongoing basis, you will end up owning some stocks for a month or less and others for many months, but very few for years. If owning stocks for only a month or two goes against your principles, then you should not write calls. If making money in the stock market, regardless of how long you hold a stock, makes more sense, then you could very well become a covered writer.

You can now get emotionally involved in your strategy rather than your stocks. All too frequently, individuals buy stocks as they buy cars and homes—on the basis of a few facts and a lot of emotions. You buy stocks in companies you like and want to see succeed. Then you become as loyal to them as to your local sports teams. The danger is that you lose sight of your whole purpose for investing and become wrapped up in the notion that by owning the company's stock, you are actually supporting it, and that if you sell it you are abandoning it.

Peter Lynch of Fidelity Magellan fame advocates buying stocks in companies you are familiar with, and that's fine. But when you get to the point that selling shares would be like betraying a friend, you have gone too far. Beyond seeking therapy, a solution to this misguided loyalty is covered writing. When you look for a stock to own for a long time, you look for a "feel good" company, something you will be pleased and proud to see on your statements for months or years to come. When you look for a covered write, you look for a stock and a call option that can get you to a specific goal in a very defined period of time, usually no more than a few months. You focus on the time and the return rather than on the emotional fix you can get from the company itself, and you see the stock as a vehicle for getting you a decent return and little more.

The other emotion surrounding stock ownership that will abate when you write covered calls is the self-doubt that accompanies every news item you read: "Are their prospects dimming? Are their markets weakening? What did that last piece of news really mean?" Do you really need to suffer this emotional roller coaster? When you put on a covered write, you will find that you are better able to remove yourself from day-to-day emotions about the underlying stock.

Your selectable universe of stocks drops from 7,500+ to about 2,300. Some may scoff at limited choice being an advantage. For an institutional investor with substantial capital to invest and a computer-driven methodology for identifying stocks, it might not be. But the situation is very different for individual investors who manage their own stock portfolios. Indeed, the prospect of having to deal with the massive and ever-changing amount of information on stocks alone is what compels many individuals to rely on brokers or professional advisers.

Choosing just from the pool of stocks with listed options, you can still create a diversified portfolio of the most actively traded stocks in America's major business categories, including manufacturing, retail, pharmaceutical, finance, energy, technology, and communications. And not only does limiting your universe in this way greatly facilitate your selection process, but you will actually become familiar enough with some of the companies to invest in them repeatedly over time without having to research them from scratch all over again.

You can rank potential returns with your computer. When you are picking stocks to buy, your challenge is to find the most attractive companies out of an enormous universe based on a huge amount of fundamental information. Some software programs, like Value Line's, enable you to screen the list for a variety of criteria, such as price, P/E, industry, or even Value Line's own rating, to help you whittle down the list. But there is no real way to rank all the companies out there by their *potential returns*.

You *can* do this, however, with covered writes. Every conceivable covered write opportunity can be ranked by its potential RIE or RU, because you can calculate exactly what those potential returns are. Then you can go down the list, examining the fundamentals to determine whether the stocks on the top of this list make sense as investments. When you find one that meets your fundamental criteria, you will know that it is already among the ones with the greatest return potential.

Some might argue that even though you can determine the maximum potential returns of all covered writes at expiration, you do not know the *likelihood* of any of them actually reaching their maximum potential, and that therefore such rankings are misleading. But, as discussed in Chapter 5, you *can* use a stock's historical volatility to determine its mathematical likelihood of reaching a specific price by a specified time.

You must review your holdings and make decisions on them each month. Covered call writing imposes a discipline that is tied to the scheduled expiration day each calendar month. If you have a covered write that is nearing expiration, you will want to see where things stand and prepare for writing another call, replacing the stock if it is called away, or rolling the position before expiration. If you don't pay attention, it is not catastrophic. Either you end up with a stock position and no call written on it, or you end up with cash to reinvest from the postassignment sale of stock. But to make the strategy work best, you will want to make these decisions as close to expiration time as possible.

Covered writing is time dependent. Its most effective implementation takes advantage of the largest rate of decrease in call option time value: the last month before expiration. If implemented this way, your investment time horizon may be no longer than one month, as previously noted. Purists of long-term fundamental investing may decry this, but for those who have difficulty knowing exactly when to sell a stock, this could be of significant benefit.

Your target selling price and time for any stock holding will be precisely determined. When you initiate stock positions for the long term, how often do you have a specific price or time objective in mind? If you do, how often do you stick to it? Probably very infrequently. And why is that? For one thing, investors don't really have a defined methodology or discipline to tell them when to sell; they make educated guesses, at best. For another, as has been stated, brokerage firms rarely issue sell recommendations. Then there is the inertia factor. Most people hold stocks too long because it is easier to do nothing than to agonize over selling. What happens all too often is that they ride a stock through a roller coaster of ups and downs and ultimately unload it, more out of frustration than from having accomplished a goal, because:

- The stock peaks and sells off considerably, at which time they decide they missed the *top* and they'd better sell before it gets worse
- The stock underperforms everything else around it, and they lose patience
- Bad news emerges, and the fundamentals sour
- They see something better or need the money.

These are all good reasons to liquidate a position, but the best, and the one you should strive for, is that the stock has achieved the profit objective you set for it.

One of the most underappreciated benefits of covered writing is that decisions about selling the underlying stock are made for you once you decide which call to sell, and that decision is much easier to make than pegging an exact price peak for the stock. The strike prices available to you when you sell covered calls are discrete: They are for the most part either 2.5 or 5 points apart. Your decision is thus relatively straightforward. If your stock is trading at $38 a share, you will most likely sell a 40 or 45 call. Once you do, that's it—your selling target is determined by the strike price, your time period is determined by the expiration, and your exit decision is enormously simplified.

You benefit each and every day in some small way from the decrease in time value. As a wasting asset, options are theoretically worth a little less each day. Of course, their prices are market-driven, not theory-driven, so they vary day-to-day, but the time pressure is always there. And over time, you can be confident that the time value of any option will decrease to zero.

The psychological benefits of this are subtle, but they are important for many investors. If you're a stock owner, you are doomed to periods of frustration and anxiety while you hold your position. Why isn't the stock moving? Why is it going down? What's really going on at the company? Some folks can live with that more easily than others, but everyone feels it—even the pros. Having time on your side will come as a refreshing change. In some options, you can see the time value deteriorate between Friday's and Monday's trading. Imagine going on vacation for a week or two and coming back to see the stock trading right where it was, but the option noticeably lower.

You get to use OPM to compound your total returns. Some years ago, actor Danny DeVito popularized the term *OPM* in the movie *Ruthless People*. His character was a businessman who boasted about using other people's money to fund a corporate acquisition. Wall Street doesn't employ the term widely, but it does employ the concept. If you prefer, just consider it the compounding effect.

If you own a stock and you write call options against it, the money you take in is yours to keep, regardless of what happens, as long as you are in fact willing to sell the stock at the strike price as the contract obligates you to do. So, in fact, it is your money, not other people's. But you are receiving it up front, at the beginning of the effective period of the obligation for which it is compensating you. It is OPM in that you have it to use even before you are required to sell anything. And you can get some of this OPM every month by writing calls against your stocks. Few investments give you monthly income, and of those, none besides covered call writing gives it to you in advance!

Receiving income up front allows you to compound your total returns, dollar cost average into more stock, or diversify your holdings. Although it is a good idea to keep some cash in your account, in case you want to close an option position or decide to roll it for a debit, the premiums you receive are yours to do with as you please. The simplest scenario involves letting them just accumulate and earn interest. This won't make you rich at today's money market rates, but even at, say, 3 percent interest per year, you would be increasing your total return by around one-third of a percentage point when you write out-of-the-money calls and up to almost a full percentage point when you write in-the-money calls.

But why settle for only a few percent from compounding when the basic strategy of covered writing is likely to generate multiples of that? In other words, why not reinvest your premiums in the strategy itself? You might not have enough for an additional round lot of stock until you generate at least several months of premiums, but once you do, you can potentially compound your returns at a rate much higher than money market interest.

You can also use the premium you receive from establishing a position to help pay for the position itself. Say you just received $4,000 from an assignment that you now need to reinvest. You find a stock that you like, but it's selling at $42, so $4,000 won't buy a full round lot. Now say there is a 45 call a few months out selling for 3 points, or $300. If you buy the stock and sell the call simultaneously, a transaction known as a buy-write, you should need to pony up only $3,900 plus transaction costs, which you can afford. (Just check with your brokerage firm to make sure it will accept buy-write orders and that you need only the net debit available in your account.)

Yet another way to use option premiums is to apply them to your debit balance if you have a margin account. If you are paying 7 percent interest on margin funds and are carrying an outstanding margin balance, using your option premiums to reduce that debit saves you 7 percent. That's the equivalent of earning 7 percent on those premiums.

Note: Some brokerages automatically place premiums from short options in a "short" account, where they are segregated from your cash or margin account. In this case, you will not have access to the money for any of the above purposes and will be lucky to receive even money market interest (at least until expiration, when the firm frees up those funds). This policy was developed to make sure that those with short positions of any kind had funds available for the eventual repurchase or closing of these positions. But covered writing is different from other types of shorting. If you are totally covered by the underlying stock, you need never repurchase the call. So this just ends up being a way for the firm to earn interest on *your* money. If your firm does this, then at least request that premiums be placed in your type 1 or type 2 account.

You can alter the risk/reward profile of your stock investments after you've initiated them. As explained in Chapter 4, rolling an option enables you to change the risk/reward character of your stock position without selling the shares. This is a tremendous benefit, albeit one that cannot easily be quantified. Still, it is easy to see how this flexibility can help you in managing your portfolio. Every time you sell a call or roll to a different position, you are changing the risk/reward profile of your underlying stock position. And if you are taking in premium when you do, you are lowering the risk by that amount. So, whether you are looking to hedge the downside, are skittish about the market environment, or want to increase your potential gains, you can adjust your position accordingly.

The volatility of your monthly returns will be lower. Despite a long-term upward bias, the stock market during much of the year either declines or exhibits a seesaw motion that doesn't appreciably change its overall performance. The Standard & Poor's 500 Index declined in 41 percent of the calendar months between 1950 and 2000. So much of the time, your stock portfolio is not working effectively for you.

A stock and covered call portfolio, in contrast, is always working for you. That's not to say it generates a positive return 100 percent of the time, but when it's not making a net positive return in any given period, it is reducing the loss for that period, and that means it is still working for you. The twenty-stock study described in Chapter 5 showed that covered writing produces smoother monthly returns than a buy-and-hold strategy: The lows are not as low and the highs are not as high. Covered writing also reduces, on average, the number of months in which you will have negative returns. The stocks in the study declined in 41 percent of the calendar months, just as the S&P 500 did during the fifty years mentioned above; continuous covered call writing on those same stocks produced negative returns in only 34 percent of the months.

You can achieve returns similar to those of the stock market with far less stress and anxiety. Let's visit the casino for this one. Bob and Rita are both playing blackjack. Bob thinks he can beat the odds by betting more money when the deck "feels" right to him. Rita uses a disciplined approach that tells her exactly when to hold, draw, double down, or split. Who do you think plays with less stress? Hint: Bob is already chastising the dealer for drawing twenty-one on the last hand and is ordering his third free cocktail. Rita is as cool as a cucumber because she knows she will win some and lose some, but that over the course of the evening, she is giving herself the best chance for success and will not have to second-guess her decisions.

When you use a disciplined approach to investing (presuming, of course, that there is a sound underlying logic to the discipline in the first place), you are generally giving yourself an advantage. It doesn't guarantee that you will always make money, but it does guarantee that you will reduce or eliminate the effect that your emotions have on your investment decisions, which is more than likely to decrease your overall degree of success.

Implementation 7

All life is the management of risk, not its elimination.

WALTER WRISTON, former CEO and chairman of Citicorp

THIS CHAPTER IS ABOUT MAKING THE TRANSITION FROM CONCEPT to reality. At this point, you should have enough information about what covered writing involves to determine how it could benefit you and whether the strategy aligns with your investment philosophy and temperament. If you are now ready to embark, this chapter will help you get started.

DECIDING ON YOUR APPROACH

Your approach to covered writing can be short term or long term, conservative or aggressive, active or passive, and as unique to you as your signature. Between the myriad different stocks you can write calls on and the different ways you can structure your positions by varying option strikes and expirations, you have the flexibility to develop a highly original implementation of the covered writing strategy in your own portfolio. What's more, you can modify this implementation over time as market conditions or personal considerations dictate. As a guide in developing your own approach to covered writing, it will help briefly to review the two basic implementations described in Chapter 4: incremental return (writing calls on existing positions) and total return (selecting stocks specifically for the purpose of covered writing).

Incremental Writing

As discussed in Chapter 4, you may be considering writing calls on part or all of an existing portfolio to generate income, hedge against a decline, establish a selling price target, or lock in gains on selected stock positions. If so, you are among the many investors and advisers who employ covered writing to generate incremental returns, a practice also referred to as *overwriting*. Underlying this approach is the philosophy that stock picking and covered call writing are independent activities — you buy stocks for their long-term potential, and you selectively write calls on them when one of the situations mentioned above occurs or the short-term picture is simply not too bright.

This can be a reasonable approach, but it contains traps for both individuals and professionals who follow it. Because of these traps, writing calls for incremental income frequently leads to disappointment when expectations are not met.

Traps Involved in Writing for Incremental Return

Some of the disadvantages of this approach were presented in Chapter 4. Primary among them is that it fosters the false notion that writing calls generates "free money" on existing stock positions. This notion fails to consider the opportunity loss that occurs when a stock position moves up beyond the strike price of its covered call and some upside potential is forgone.

Other traps to watch out for are discussed here. The biggest potential problems stem from the fact that those writing calls for incremental return tend to do so based not on scientific factors but on subjective "feelings" that although a stock has an attractive long-term upside, its near-term prospects are not great. This can lead to mistakes such as the following:

- **Writing calls at the wrong times.** Incremental writers tend to write calls intermittently, based on a stock's past behavior rather than on its anticipated behavior. An example of this is writing calls on a stock that has not moved appreciably in some time. If the stock has been relatively flat for several months, its volatility, and hence the premiums of calls written on it, will be somewhat lower than usual. If it continues flat, then writing a call could prove beneficial, but if it breaks out of its doldrums on the upside, you may have given up some of that upside for a lower-than-usual amount of call premium.

    There is a similar tendency not to write calls on a stock that is moving steadily up. Yet this is when both volatility and the price of the underlying stock may provide you with the best opportunities to capture option premium and also realize gains on the stock. The bottom line is that you can never know for sure whether writing a call will be more beneficial than simply holding the stock during the same period until expiration. So if you're waiting to decide whether to write, you are basing your decision on past performance rather than what may happen before the next expiration.

- **Believing you can time the market.** If you sell calls only when you "feel it is safe" (that is, when you believe your stock won't rise enough to be called away), you are in dangerous waters. Few people succeed at this assessment consistently over time, particularly if they are operating largely on gut feelings. Say you buy a stock at $40 because you believe it will be priced between $60 and $70 in a year or so. Six months later, the stock is trading at $46. You decide that at the rate it's been moving, you can write a two-month call option at a strike of 50 for, say, 1.50 and not have to worry about your shares being called away. One month later, the stock breaks out and runs to $54. Stocks rarely exhibit a nice steady increase each month just to accommodate your strategy. So, your stock is on track to achieve your long-term objective, but you have given up any appreciation above $50 for another month. You can recapture this appreciation by rolling up and out, but the point is that you tried to time the market with your covered write and it did not work to your benefit. Meanwhile, you elected not to write during the first six months, when you could have taken in premiums at the 45 or 50 strike prices without being called away.

The Total-Return Approach

The alternative to writing for incremental return is to specifically select stocks that are attractive as covered writes, seeking total return from stock appreciation plus a continuous flow of option premium. In doing so, you concentrate your research on stocks that have listed options and determine which are attractive not just on their own merits, but in combination with their call options. This could mean rejecting a stock that you like fundamentally but for which there are no options, or choosing to establish a covered write on a stock that you might not have invested in by itself.

There is a substantial difference in orientation between the incremental and the total-return approaches. Stock selection is entirely different, timing is different, and ongoing portfolio management is different. If you are astute, you might be able to mix the two strategies, but when you do, you subject yourself to the traps inherent in both.

Total-return investors don't have to guess when it might be appropriate to write a call. Their approach is predicated on the strategy's ability, over time, to produce consistent returns without guesswork. They can use fundamental research to help pick stocks, but not in the same way—or with the same objective—as the incremental writer. Thus, the objective in total return is not to buy a stock for $40 that has the potential to trade between $60 and $70 in one or two years. The objective is to buy a stock at $40 and write a 40 or 45 call based on the judgment that the stock is likely at least to remain where it is, if not go higher, in the next month or so. There is therefore a stronger need for the investor to feel confident that the stock won't drop to $30 in the next month, than that it will attain the far more ambitious (and often more elusive) goal of rising to $60 in the next year. A solid fundamental picture helps lower the possibility of a sharp decline. But covered writers should also study technical trends and support and resistance points to determine likely scenarios for the duration of their option positions.

Traps in the Total-Return Approach

Like the incremental-income approach, the total-return approach also has its traps. Key among them are the following:

- **Writing the highest premium.** If you are looking for covered writing opportunities, you will see numerous situations in which option premiums appear exorbitant and offer highly attractive potential returns. The problem is that very often these candidates are highly volatile stocks or stocks that have speculative fever built into their prices. High premiums can have any number of causes. They may even be a bearish indicator. When there is the possibility of a downside move—say, in the event the company is named in a substantial lawsuit—put options are likely to increase in value as large stakeholders buy them to protect their positions. In such situations, arbitrage among the puts, calls, and the underlying stock will generally cause the call premiums to rise as well. (This process is explained in more detail in Chapter 8.) In other words, the calls increase in value as a result of the likelihood that the stock will decline. If you go after these situations, you may be in for more of a ride than you bargained for.
- **Too much focus on the option, not enough on the stock.** When writing covered calls, it's easy to lose sight of the fact that the stock is your main investment and that it holds virtually all your downside risk. An attractive premium should always be evaluated in relation to the underlying stock's prospects. You should keep in mind that if the share price declines, you can lose money despite the premium income (although still less than if you owned the stock by itself).

This typically occurs with volatile stocks that have options two or three strike prices above the current share price whose premiums seem high. Say such a stock is trading at $46 and you can get 1.50 for a two-month call at the 55 strike price. This may provide a whopping return if exercised, but it will not offset the downside risk of the stock trading below $44.50.

■ **Unrealistic expectations for returns if exercised.** When looking for covered writes and ranking them by potential return, you will see some huge potential RIEs (returns if exercised). This can occur with any highly volatile stock that has call options with strike prices well above where the shares are currently trading. The calls often provide attractive premiums while still allowing significant upside gains on the stock before being assigned. It is easy in such situations to lose sight of the fact that volatile stocks present greater downside risk as well. In the example above, the return if exercised for the 55 strike call would be 22.8 percent ($9 on the stock plus $1.50 for the call, divided by the purchase price of $46) in two months. Sounds terrific. But what is the reasonable likelihood of the stock reaching that strike price in 60 days? The return if unchanged on this position is only 3.2 percent.

■ **Not writing continuously.** Total-return writers can fall into the same trap incremental writers face—that of trying to guess when to write and when not to. If you buy a stock because it represents an attractive covered write and then decide not to write another call when the first one expires, you are defeating the purpose of selecting that stock to begin with. Even in the above example, where the static return was 3.2 percent, by not writing that call, you would be losing out on premium that annualizes to more than 19 percent. The same observation holds for situations where you are assigned but do not reinvest your proceeds in a new position right away.

The main point here is that many of the benefits that accrue from covered writing stem from the discipline that the strategy imposes. You can mix strategies or even modify your strategy over time, but if you are not clear about your implementation, chances are you will have difficulty maintaining discipline and will fall into one or more of the traps mentioned above. Whether you are writing for incremental return or total return, your overall success in and satisfaction with covered writing are greatest when you are clear about your implementation and mindful of the traps.

ARE YOU A FUNDAMENTALIST OR A TECHNICIAN?

As noted above, a major difference between writing for incremental income and writing for total return is the way stocks are selected. This difference coincides with the distinction between two camps of stock market analysis: fundamental and technical. Investors tend to fall decidedly into one camp or the other. It is important to understand what your orientation is, since that will determine which approach to covered writing suits your style best.

Fundamental analysis is the backbone of investment research. Analysts look at company financials, business trends, characteristics of the target market, growth rates, competitive position—just about anything that has a direct impact on the general health and future prospects of the business, including external factors like labor, legal, or regulatory issues and how much the company might be worth to another company. Their objective is to reduce this information to a set of earnings projections and recommend whether investors should buy, hold, or sell the stock accordingly. These recommendations are made with an eye to the long term—at least several quarters if not a year or more—and are arrived at largely without regard for what the overall market is doing. Fundamental analysis is thus not particularly adept at telling you how the stock might behave in the next month or two.

Technical analysis is almost the exact opposite of fundamental analysis. Technical analysts could care less whether a company has earnings or even a product. Their conclusions are short term, concerned with where a stock (or sector or entire stock market) is going in the next few months at most. To reach these conclusions, those taking a technical approach study charts and graphs representing stock price movements, analyze purchase and sale statistics, and draw trend lines. The assumption is that the patterns of buyer and seller behavior revealed by their analyses can provide clues as to where individual stocks and the overall averages are going. A chart, for example, can offer valuable insights into—although no guarantees on—whether a trend is in place and where support levels (prices at which buyers have previously shown willingness to buy if the stock is declining) exist. A number of Internet sites specialize in charts, including BigCharts.com and Stockcharts.com, both of which offer free charting capabilities; Stockcharts.com also has a chart school with loads of free education.

As a covered writer, you need to reconcile your approach with your preferred stock-selection technique. If you pick stocks based on long-term fundamentals, you are in synch with the incremental approach. But fundamental analysis will not help you determine when to write the calls. For that you need to consider technical factors. Otherwise, you will resort to intuition and may fall into the trap of "believing you can time the market." If you intend to adopt a total-return approach and you generally select stocks using technical analysis, you may fall into the trap of "writing the highest premium" and ignoring sound fundamentals. The point is that regardless of whether you approach covered writing from the incremental or the total-return perspective, you will be best served by using some combination of both fundamental and technical analysis in your decisions.

SELECTING STOCK POSITIONS

If you are in the incremental camp with regard to covered writing, your process for selecting stocks may be based on long-term fundamentals, recommendations from your broker, newsletters, or some other source. Whatever information you consult, you are choosing stocks on their merits as long-term holdings rather than on their merits as covered writes.

By contrast, if you are going to become a total-return covered writer, your stock selection process will be somewhat different from any you have used before. You may be interested in positive long-term fundamentals, but your primary focus is on identifying stocks that have calls with attractive premiums as well as a high probability of reaching or staying above the option's strike price by expiration. This process is described below.

Whichever camp you choose to be in, you can search for stocks in two different ways: by using your usual sources for equity ideas and simply passing over those without options, or by specifically looking through stocks with options for attractive covered writes and passing on any that have questionable fundamentals or that don't suit your risk tolerance. It is generally advisable to confine your search to stocks with options, since this gives you the most flexibility. There is nothing, however, that says you cannot use both of these methods to identify potential opportunities.

Searching All Stocks

Now that some 2,300 stocks have listed options, you will find that whether your source for stock ideas is your broker's recommended list, an independent service such as Standard & Poor's, Moody's, Value Line, or Morningstar, or a stock picker's newsletter, you generally don't have to go very far down the list to find a stock with listed options. In fact, many of the sources named above will indicate the existence of options right in a stock's description.

Once you have identified stocks you like, the next step is to go online to obtain current pricing and view the option *chains*, also sometimes called *option strings* or *montages*. (Chapter 9 lists several online services together with examples of chains and other information they provide.) An option chain is a summary table that lists all of the available options on a particular stock. A quick glance can usually tell you whether the stock meets your criteria and, if so, which call option you should zero in on. From the chain, you are able to determine:

- **Available months and strike prices, together with premiums.** Depending on where a stock is trading, you may or may not find something to write. If you like one-month writes, for example, and the shares are trading at $14.50, you may feel that the 15 strike doesn't offer enough upside potential on the stock and that the 17.5 or 20 strike has too little premium. You might then move on to the next expiration month or check a related stock to see if the choices are more to your liking. If you do see option opportunities that appear attractive, you should note the symbol so that you don't have go to a full option chain the next time you want to obtain a quote on that option or track it.

■ **Liquidity.** You determine liquidity by looking at the daily trading volume and the open interest. All listed options have active quotes showing at what prices you can buy or sell them. But the less liquid ones tend to have larger spreads between the bid and ask prices. That means you'll receive a little less when you sell and pay a little more when you buy than if the market were more efficient.

Illiquidity should be one of the reasons you reject a stock from consideration. The cost difference between bid and offer for a nonliquid option may be only 0.05 or 0.10 points, but it could also be as much as 0.60 or more. Even a quarter of a point (0.25) difference, although it may not seem like much, is equivalent to three full points on an annualized basis. That's $300 on a single contract. On a round lot of a $20 stock, that represents a 15 percent annualized return! When a call option has very low liquidity and a spread of more than, say, 0.25 to 0.30, you should probably look for another stock for your covered write. If you already own the stock and are writing incrementally, use a limit order to try to get a price somewhere between the bid and the offer.

You can use the near-month at-the-money call as a benchmark, since the farther out in time and the farther away from the current stock price you go, the less liquid the options. There is no magic number for determining an acceptable amount of liquidity, but as a rule of thumb if an option trades fewer than 50 contracts a day or has fewer than 500 contracts of open interest, yellow caution flags should go up. It doesn't mean you can never write these contracts. You should just pay attention to the bid-ask spread and make sure you can get a price that you feel is fair, given where the stock is trading.

Note that when you are obtaining an option quote, you should not necessarily worry about an abnormally large spread between bid and offer if it occurs outside normal trading hours. The quotes posted at the end of the day for both stocks and options may not reflect the bids and offers you will see during the trading day.

▪ **Value.** In addition to the basic quote and symbol, at least some option chains will also list an option's hypothetical value according to the Black-Scholes formula. From this you can determine whether the calls on your selected stock are trading above or below their theoretical values. This not only helps you in your stock selection—you will generally want to identify stocks whose calls have premiums higher than their theoretical values—but can also indicate if something is going on with the company of which you should be aware. If, for example, option premiums are quite a bit above the theoretical value and volume is much higher than normal, you should check recent news on the company for some event that could be causing this aberration. When no reason is apparent for the high premiums, you may want to avoid the stock, since it could be subject to a sharp move one way or the other.

Searching Specifically for Covered Writes

An efficient way to select stocks for covered writing is to use a software package or Internet-based service that is designed to screen all the available covered writes. (These services are discussed in Chapter 9.) In this manner, you can literally rank the entire listed option universe according to either returns unchanged (RU) or returns if exercised (RIEs). Generally, you would begin by setting up a filter for stocks trading within a certain price range or at a certain price-to-earning ratio, or for some other criterion. Once you have your list, you can rank the members by return and look at the top situations to decide whether they are worth examining further.

Here are some characteristics to look for in selecting stocks for covered writing:

▪ **High-quality fundamentals with stable performance.** It is good to keep an eye on a handful of high-quality companies in stable industries that you can count on to give you attractive premiums plus the possibility of appreciation. These are equivalent to the types of stocks brokers recommend as "core holdings." In fact, some of them probably are the same stocks. If you have four or five companies such as Citigroup, Merck, and Microsoft, say, that you like as long-term investments, then all you need to do is check to see which offer a good balance between stock price and call premium in a given month, and you've got yourself a covered write candidate.

▪ **Companies with potential that may take a while to develop.** At one time or another, you've probably stuck a long shot in your portfolio—a company you think could be the next Microsoft, develop the cure for cancer, or figure out a way to really make money off the Internet. You know you may have to hold it for a while, but you buy it because you feel confident it has well above-average long-term potential. But you also know that the potentially big payoff may not happen for a year or two. Some of these may be quiet little companies that are not widely followed and whose options are not very liquid. Those would not make attractive covered writes. Others, however, are already getting attention and have lots of call premium you can sell. These can make very attractive covered writes in the short term, due largely to their options.

▪ **High option premiums.** These are going to be associated with more volatile stocks, so you need to do a little more homework on them to arrive at the appropriate candidates for call writes. Frequently, they are *situation* stocks—subjects of news or rumors. But just as often they are simply stocks that move around a lot and therefore carry more premium in their options. If there is fairly widespread talk of a merger or acquisition, you may see very nice call premiums, but you are also likely to see a stock that is already priced high. In that case, the price will be vulnerable to a pullback if the company denies it is in talks or if nothing happens by the expected time. Another high-premium situation involves stocks that have been hammered by bad news. The drop increases the stock's volatility, which can be reflected in higher-than-usual call premiums. A stock that has fallen sharply can thus be very attractive for a covered writer. However, here, too, you run the risk that a lower share price is warranted by the news or that it may fall even farther.

■ **Stocks with favorable technicals, as revealed in charts.** If you are a chart watcher, you will see stocks that are *breaking out* or *reversing* or showing positive *momentum*. These technical signals indicate that the share price could be poised to rise and therefore point to attractive write situations. If you are going to write covered calls and are not in the habit of using technical analysis, it's a good idea to spend some time familiarizing yourself with this useful approach for gaining insight into price movement.

SELECTING CALLS TO WRITE

Depending on the stock, it's possible that you could have anywhere from 10 to 100 call options to choose from at any one time. However, the pool decreases quickly when you limit the candidates to those that match your game plan. If you like to write at-the-money calls with one or two months to expiration, you would zero in on these. If you are writing for incremental return on a stock you already own, you will probably start with the highest strike price available and work down from this or move out in time until you find a call with sufficient premium.

Which Strike Price?

The strike price decision essentially grows out of your risk posture and will generally boil down to a choice between one or two strikes. The vast majority of covered calls that are written are for the strike closest to the current share price, whether in- or out-of-the-money. The following table illustrates how different prices can correspond to different strategies, using a September-expiration covered call written on Dell Computer in mid-August, when the stock was trading at $26.25.

Strike Price	Option Price	Strategy
Sep 22.5 call	4.40	This is the ultraconservative strike. You earn only 0.65 of time premium before commission—a 2.5% gain for 39 days. It probably won't pay for a small account that holds only a few hundred shares. But for someone with a larger account, paying very low commissions, who wants plenty of downside protection (in this case, nearly 17%), this could be the preferable strike.
Sep 25 call	2.50	This strike is still relatively conservative. The option pays 1.25 of time value before commission—a 4.8% return—and still provides almost 10% downside protection.
Sep 27.5 call	1.10	This is the modest-risk covered write and the one most writers would probably select at this stock price. It offers almost as much static gain as the 25 strike (4.1%), and although the downside protection drops to the same 4.1%, the upside potential (RIE) jumps to nearly 9%, before commission, for the 39 days.
Sep 30 call	0.30	This is the aggressive covered write, with only a marginal (1.1%) static return. It is almost like simply owning the stock, because there is so little downside protection. Like the ultraconservative strike, it wouldn't really pay at low volume, since you are only getting $30 per contract, less commission. Even for large accounts or investors writing for incremental return, such a write is of questionable benefit.

Bear in mind that while the situation illustrated in the table is typical of the tradeoffs between in-the-money and out-of-the-money calls, the scenario is dynamic. A $1 move up or down in share price could easily change which call you write or even cause you to reject writing on that stock at all. Many times you will like a stock but not find a call that suits you. The following month, or the following week, the same stock may offer a much more attractive write. Much of this variation in attractiveness has to do with where the stock is trading relative to the strike prices of its options. It is most likely to happen with stocks priced between $30 and $50, whose options have strike prices in $5 increments. Say you prefer covered writes where the underlying stock is trading one or two dollars below the strike price. If a stock you like is trading at $38, for example, you most likely would be comfortable with the amount of premium that the 40 strike offers, and you would still have some upside potential in the stock. The 35 call would probably be too far in the money to offer a high enough return and would offer no upside in the stock at all, while the 45 strike might not provide enough premium. But if the stock is trading at $35.50, none of the available strikes may suit you, and you may decide to write on a different stock for the present. Next month, the first stock may be exactly where you want it. How you choose between in-the-money and out-of-the-money calls is up to you. There are good rationales for both at different times, and even for using both at the same time on different stocks. It all comes down to how much of a stock's upside potential for the period you are willing to trade away for more return. Be advised, however, that if you find yourself always selling the in-the-money calls, you may not be allowing yourself enough upside potential in the long run to offset the risks on the downside. While downside protection is often advantageous, if you believe that stocks do in fact have a long-term upward bias, you should profit from that growth if possible.

Which Expiration Month?

Time premium is the component of an option's total premium that diminishes over time, and as a call writer, this decay is what makes you money. Chapter 5 explained that time premium decays faster as an option approaches its expiration. That means that all other things being equal, to take the most advantage of the dissipation in time value of call options, writers are best served by writing the near-month option whenever possible. That is why so much of this book uses examples that are one to two months in duration. You can frequently find very attractive covered writes even in the last one to three weeks before an expiration. Say you are assigned on a position and have money to reinvest but can't find anything in the next expiration month you really like. A week later, with only three weeks to go before that next expiration, you might be surprised at some of the opportunities that surface for either that month or the next one out.

Although some people find it difficult to take what might be considered such a short-term perspective, it has some key advantages:

- Over time, you take in more time premium per day in your positions, thereby enhancing your overall returns.
- You have much more flexibility to roll your option positions should you decide to. (By writing in the nearest month, you have the most other months to roll out to and the greatest likelihood of rolling for a credit.)
- You have more flexibility to adjust to market conditions or seize on opportunities that arise. (You're tying your money up for less time.)
- You don't ride positions too long because you're forced to reevaluate your positions every month.

If you have idle funds or extra buying power in your account, there is nothing wrong in putting on a covered write just a week or even a few days before option expiration. Some people, however, sell out-of-the-money calls on the last trading day before they expire without buying or owning the underlying stock, reasoning that with expiration so near, they needn't incur the expense and risk of owning the shares. This is a temptation you should resist. True, calls on volatile stocks can carry premiums of 0.10, 0.20, or more with only a few hours of trading left and the stock selling several points below the strike price. But unless you buy the underlying stock, these are considered naked calls, even if you write them only a day before they expire. This would represent an account violation if you aren't approved for naked call writing. In addition, you won't be a happy camper if big news about the company is announced after the close that day, causing you to be assigned on stock you don't own, which opens much higher on Monday morning.

The only real consequence of a short-term approach is that you will pay more commissions, since you are writing more often. How much of an impact this will have on your returns depends on the fee structure of the brokerage you use.

GETTING YOUR DUCKS IN A ROW WITH YOUR BROKERAGE

If you are going to write options and have never done so before, you need to address how to structure your relationship with your brokerage. This involves not only your choice of firm but what services you will get from it and what you will do yourself. You can set up a covered writing account at just about any National Association of Securities Dealers (NASD) member securities firm, whether it's a full-service brokerage, a discount firm, or an online broker, but there are several factors you should consider in making your choice.

Full-Service versus Discount Brokers

Chapter 5 illustrated the effect of commissions on the returns from covered writing. The difference between standard full-service rates and discounted commissions can be considerable and can make the difference in whether or not covered writing is worth implementing in your account. If you are paying a full-service commission (typically somewhere around 1 to 3 percent of the principal amount to buy or sell stock), covered writing will be prohibitively expensive. Think of it this way: If your maximum gain for a one-month covered write is 3 to 5 percent and you have to pay 1 to 2 percent in commissions each way, you are eating up almost all of your potential gain with transaction costs. You would need to obtain a discount of 25 to 40 percent or more off the standard full-service rates to make the transaction worthwhile. Get some sample quotes on the amounts and prices of both stocks and options you might be considering and do some math to see if it pays. If you can get a fixed-fee account for around 2 percent a year from your full-service broker, you can see how advantageous that would be.

Commissions are not the same at all "discount brokers," but they will all be far more favorable than full-service rates. Whether you pay $9.99, $14.99, $19.99, or even $29.99 for buying 400 shares of a $25 stock ($10,000 in principal), you are still paying a fraction of a percent in commission. Remember to consider your minimum transaction costs, though, particularly with options. There is not much sense in selling two option contracts at 0.25 ($50) if you are paying a $29 minimum commission just to keep the remaining $21.

One advantage of a full-service firm is that it is more likely to be able to do a covered write as a single buy-write order. As noted in Chapter 4, a buy-write is an order to execute a stock purchase and option sale as a single transaction. You specify the net debit price—equal to the cost of the stock less the call option premium—and your brokerage firm executes the combined transaction when both positions can be obtained at your price, charging the regular commissions. (Buy-write orders are discussed in more detail later in the chapter.) Another advantage of full-service firms is that you get a dedicated representative who provides you with personal service. If you do not have the time or inclination to go online and check your holdings every few days or so, it is very helpful to have a broker who can call you if there is news you should know about or with new ideas. In addition, reps at the full-service firms have real-time quotes and may even be able to get detailed quotes at different exchanges or from multiple market makers. While not essential, this capability can be useful, especially if you are picky about execution prices or if you are dealing in large positions.

However, many reps, even though Series 7 licensed (the standard NASD requirement for all brokers who solicit securities sales), simply do not "do" options. If your rep generally does not handle options for clients, do your covered writing elsewhere. You should be up front and ask. If you are not confident in his knowledge, discuss a few potential ideas and get a few quotes on current option prices to see if he can provide the kind of information you will need. Also, be prepared for some reps to discourage you from using options, even if you intend only to write covered calls. Many prefer not to deal with options at all, and they may be coached by their firms to avoid them. If one rep cannot support you in your covered writing strategy, then you ought to find someone else who can.

Even if your rep is option fluent, you should not necessarily assume that he or she will be focused on looking for covered writing ideas. Brokers have a lot of products on which to keep current. Relying on them to supply stock ideas is one thing, but relying on them to call when they see a good covered write or when it might be time to roll your position is another. In addition, brokerage firm research departments do not, as a rule, issue covered writing commentary. Unless your rep does covered writing for a number of other clients, you may need to supplement his services with research of your own.

Online Brokers

Online brokerage accounts work well for covered writing, especially for the more independent investor. The commission structures are low, and you can get quotes, news, and portfolio information online. Online brokers are likely to provide real-time option information, although some will provide prices with a fifteen- or twenty-minute delay unless you pay extra or qualify through your trading volume. Most online firms also allow you to call in an order. This provides you with a back-up when you are traveling and can't go online. Sometimes, however, phone orders cost a few dollars more. Online reps are transaction-oriented, so they should all be stock and option savvy, although they do not offer advice or ideas.

Financial Planners

If you deal with a financial planner or adviser who focuses primarily on products such as mutual funds or insurance, even if he or she is able to transact *occasional* stock purchases for you, you shouldn't use this relationship for covered writing. Most planners and advisers simply are not equipped to handle stock and option transactions, and many do not even have the NASD Series 7 license to do so. Don't be bashful about clarifying whether your adviser has the capability to buy or sell options on your behalf. Ask for a stock and an option quote. If your adviser is not able to do that from his desk, conduct your covered writing elsewhere.

Which Account to Use?

You can set up a covered call writing portfolio in either a cash account or a margin account. Margin accounts will give you more flexibility, but cash accounts work fine, too. To use an existing account for your covered writing portfolio, you would simply need to fill out the option agreement for that account and get an approval from your brokerage firm. If there are additional stocks, bonds, or other securities in the account, they will not be affected by your covered writing activities.

Firms may or may not allow covered options writing in a custodial account, although it would actually be a sensible long-term strategy to use for a child's education savings account, for example. You'll have to ask your firm about that possibility. Also, be advised that if you have an account in joint names, both parties will have to sign the option agreement.

It is permissible to write covered options in IRAs and other self-directed retirement accounts, unless your brokerage firm has an internal rule prohibiting it. The IRS allows it, and most brokerage firms do as well. Because gains in retirement accounts are not taxed until removed (or not taxed at all, if in Roth IRAs), these accounts are very attractive places to do covered writing.

Just remember, any stock on which you wish to write calls must be in the same account as the options you write. So if you are opening a new account somewhere for covered writing and your stock is being transferred into it from another firm, you will need to wait until the stock is duly recorded in the new account before writing against it.

Writing Calls on Your Employer's Stock

You may have accumulated stock in your employer through an employee benefit program such as a stock purchase plan or stock grants. You might also have company stock in your 401(k) or other retirement plan. If it is a listed stock with options available, you may be able to write calls on it. The key issues are where the stock is held and, of course, whether or not you are fully vested in it.

Sometimes the stock vests (essentially, becomes yours) only after you have been at the company for a specified period of time. Until it vests, you cannot do anything with it. Once it is yours free and clear, the next question is whether you want to write covered calls on part or all of your position. If you have a sizable amount of company stock, writing calls on it could be very worthwhile over time, but your decision should be based on how much you have, whether you are willing to sell part or all of it, tax consequences, and so on.

If you do decide you want to write calls on the stock, it will have to be in an account in your name. If it is held for you in escrow or in an account in the company's name, for example, it will need to be transferred to an account in your name. If your company stock is held in a 401(k) plan, you will need to see whether the plan administrator allows covered option writing or whether you can transfer your company stock to a self-directed IRA. (When you leave an employer, for instance, you have the right by law to transfer assets in your 401(k) to a self-directed IRA account.)

Keeping Records

Your brokerage firm will send you trade confirmations and monthly statements, on paper or by e-mail. These documents are complete and detailed, but they are generally deficient for covered writing in two ways:

- They do not combine the stock and option holdings to show the performance of individual covered writing positions.
- They usually do not provide records of your transactions in the form you will need to report them for tax purposes.

Brokerage records report only on individual positions. Thus, if you are interested in what you gained or lost from a specific *combination* of a long stock position and one or more short call positions, you need to figure it out on your own. In addition, when filing your state and federal tax returns at the end of the year, you will need to report your trades on a Schedule D, and your broker is not likely to provide the information in that form.

Both of these deficiencies can be overcome by creating a spreadsheet in Microsoft Excel or other spreadsheet application and keeping a regular log in it of your covered writing activities. Once you create the spreadsheet, updating it from trade confirmations or monthly statements is quite simple. At the end of the year, the file can be printed and attached to your other tax forms. (A sample of an Excel spreadsheet for this purpose is included in Appendix B.)

PLACING ORDERS

Executions are more important to a covered writer than to a long-term stock buyer. If you're buying a stock with the intention of holding it for many months, $0.10 or $0.15 per order placed might not be worth fretting about. But in covered writing, you will buy and sell much more frequently during the year, and even a difference of $0.10 or $0.15 on a regular basis can add up to a substantial amount. Consequently, the type of order you use to initiate your positions can have a significant impact on your overall returns.

Market and Limit Orders

If you use market orders for your writes, you are guaranteed immediate execution, but your order will be filled at the current offer price. Using limit orders (specifying your price) will save you money on your stock and option trades, but you risk not having them filled, and eventually you may be forced to settle for a less-optimal price because the market has moved away from you. Also, with a limit order you can receive a partial fill, buying or selling only a fraction of the shares you wanted to. To avoid this, you need to stipulate "all-or-none." Here are some suggestions on how to enter your stock and option orders:

▪ Use limit orders when first purchasing the stock. You have nothing to lose if you don't get your price right away, and you have the most flexibility at this time. You will do much better saving a point or two on the stock than 0.10 or 0.15 of a point on the option. You can even decide to put a limit order in at a lower price than where the stock is currently trading (either for the day or as a "good till canceled"), in hopes of buying it cheaper.

▪ Try to make your stock purchases in the middle of the trading day (11 A.M. to 2 P.M. Eastern Time), when the stock and its options are somewhat less likely to be moving rapidly one way or the other. Try to avoid the first and last half-hours of the trading day, since they can be much more volatile.

▪ When selling your covered calls, use a limit order if you are able to watch how they are trading using real-time quotes. Place your order about midway between the bid and ask prices for the options. Bear in mind, however, that unlike stocks, which trade in $0.01 increments, options trade in increments of 0.05 if priced under 3.00, and of 0.10 if priced over 3.00. (Those trading exactly at 3.00 straddle the two conventions: You could see bids of, say, 2.90 or 2.95, but the offer would have to be 3.00, 3.10, or 3.20.)

▪ Selling a relatively illiquid option with a wide spread presents a challenge. Try a limit order between the quotes first. If there are no trades in the option and the stock trades down, however, your order may not get filled at all unless you change to a market order or to a limit at a lower price. Say an option you're trying to sell is quoted at 0.80 to 1.20, and the last trade was made at 1.00. You might begin by placing a limit order at 1.00 or even 1.10. Should someone place a market order to buy, you will have the best offer. If, however, you wait for a while and no trades take place, you might change your limit order to 0.90. Chances are, you'll do better than the 0.80 you'd have received by placing a market order initially. But it's possible you will sit for hours with no execution. Meanwhile, you need to keep an eye out for a decline in the stock and a lowering of the 0.80 bid.

■ If you cannot get real-time quotes or cannot be available if your broker calls, use market orders for the call positions, but steer clear of covered writes that involve illiquid options.

Stop Orders

A stop order is an order to buy or sell once a certain price is reached—say, buy 200 XYZ at 26 stop. This type of order is not usually appropriate for options, but it may be used for stocks—for instance, if you want to own a stock only if it *breaks out* above a certain price or sell it if it *breaks down* below a certain level. The expectation is that if it does break out, it will run a good bit further in the same direction. A stop order is not recommended on the sell side when you have a covered write, since it would leave you with a naked call option position when executed. Keep in mind that once a stop order is triggered, it becomes an immediate market order unless you stipulate a *stop limit price.* For example, the stop order to buy XYZ becomes a market purchase order as soon as the shares reach $26 or higher, unless you indicate a limit price. By placing a limit of, say, $26.50, you avoid the situation in which the stock opens 2 or 3 points higher one morning and you have to buy it at $28 or more.

Buy-Write Orders

Buy-write orders are useful when you cannot watch the markets at all during the trading day. Not every firm accepts these orders, however, and some online accounts may not be able to handle them in their online order templates.

A buy-write order instructs the broker to acquire the stock and sell the call only if the net price of the two together meets your limit. This guarantees that the position is put on at the cost you want or not at all, and the firm absorbs the responsibility for putting on both sides. Use a net price that is based on the last trades for the stock and the options rather than taking the offer on the stock and the bid on the option. (If you do the latter, you might as well just put in two separate market orders at the same time.) The broker can transact the two components at any combination of prices that meets your net limit. If the firm can buy stock at the current offering price and sell the call at the current bid price to meet your net price, the order will be filled quickly. If you are trying to get a better price, however, you'll have to be patient.

Example:
Buy 100 ABC at $29.50
Sell 1 ABC Mar 30 call at 1.50
Net debit = $28.

In this example, you are trying to put on a covered write for a net debit of $28. You may, in fact, get an execution at $29.25 for the stock and 1.25 for the option, but as long as you net $28, it really shouldn't matter. You are still investing the same amount of money. Remember that your net price is just for the positions themselves. Transaction costs will be added to both sides.

Using Spread Orders When Rolling

A *spread position* is one that involves both a long and a short option position of the same type on the same stock—for example, the position might be long 5 ABC April 50 calls and short 5 ABC April 55 calls. A spread position can be initiated via a *spread order,* in which you simultaneously execute both the buy and the sell sides for a net price (as you do with a buy-write). You might, for instance, put in an order to buy 5 XYZ Aug 25 calls and sell 5 XYZ September 25 calls for a net price of 2 points credit. (Specifying a debit or credit helps ensure that the broker understands which is the buy side and which is the sell side.) As a covered writer, you won't put on spread positions, but when you are rolling one covered call to another, you can use a spread order to simultaneously buy one option to close and sell another to open.

Spread orders are always limit orders; if they were market orders, nothing would be served by combining the two parts into a single transaction. As with the buy-write, your broker can execute the two sides at any combination of prices that meets your net price. In the spread order described above, for example, the firm could transact the buy side at 3 and the sell side at 5 for a 2-point net credit.

RISKS

As my Army Jump School instructor told us in the final class before our big parachute jump: "Now, here's what you need to know if your chute doesn't open."

- **Market risk.** Covered writers need to remember that they are stockholders and are subject to the market risk of their stock positions—that is, the risk posed by the fact that their shares will fluctuate in price and that this movement is beyond their control. The sale of call options may offset part, but never all, of that risk.

  After you buy a stock at $37.5 and sell a 40 call, the share price is as likely to drop to $35 as it is to rise above $40 by expiration. This is a fact of life for stock investors and does not change when you write calls. The calls do smooth the net effect of these fluctuations, but they do not affect the chances of them occurring.
- **Trading risk.** Trading risk relates to the fact that prices can move while you are trying to execute the two parts of your covered write. Placing your stock and option orders as closely together in time as possible will mitigate this risk, but if you intentionally wait between orders, hoping for a better price, you increase the danger of getting a worse one.
- **Trading halts.** Trading on listed options is always halted when trading on the underlying stock is halted. This might happen after an announcement that significantly affects the share price, to allow the news to be digested and orders to be balanced. Option trading also can be halted for external reasons, such as a power failure on the exchange floor or other such calamity. Usually, these interruptions are brief, but there is no way to predict their occurrence or duration.

  When trading is halted on a listed option, holders still have the right to exercise, and writers must fulfill their contracts. You cannot, however, go into the marketplace and close out your position. A trading halt is typically a temporary situation and not a major problem for covered call writers. Option holders, on the other hand, can be forced to exercise if they are unable to sell their options in the open market. Consider the following, somewhat extreme, example: You own XYZ stock and have written the March 55 call. It is Thursday before March expiration and a hostile takeover offer has been made for XYZ at $60. Trading in the stock is halted at $53 and does not reopen on Friday. Heavy speculation will occur on the upside, but until the stock trades, holders of the XYZ March 55 call will not know whether or not to exercise. If they feel the stock will open on Monday above $55, the holders will want to own it and will have to exercise. Otherwise, the call will expire worthless. On the other hand, they may feel the stock will settle back first, giving them time to buy it below $55 on Monday or whenever trading reopens. Some holders may thus choose to exercise while others may not. That means you may be assigned or you may not. Either way, though, the situation has not hurt you, except that it prevented you from closing your position before expiration.

An underlying stock can also be delisted, or it may no longer meet the minimum criteria for having listed options—it may fall below $5, for instance. In this event, no new options would be issued, and while existing ones may continue to trade, there may be little or no liquidity. Such options can, however, still be exercised.

BASIC TAX RULES FOR OPTIONS

If you do your covered writing in a qualified retirement account, such as a 401(k) or self-directed IRA, you don't have to worry about the tax consequences. But if you use a regular taxable brokerage account, you'll have an extra burden at tax time simply from having to account for all of your stock and option transactions in the prior year. In addition, you'll need to be aware of some rules that apply to covered writing. This section looks at those rules. Bear in mind, though, that tax rules can change. Also, you may be affected by other, more broadly directed tax rules beyond those mentioned here. We advise that you consult the latest IRS documentation or your tax adviser before filing your taxes. And if you're considering a strategy specifically designed to defer taxes, consult a tax adviser *before* implementing it.

- **Capital gains and losses from options are subject to taxes, just as those from stock are, and the holding period is the same.** You may consider option premiums as *income*, but the IRS treats them as capital assets. Currently, you have to hold an asset for at least one year in order for a gain on its sale to qualify for the lower tax rate charged on long-term capital gains. Since the longest duration for conventional listed options is nine months, their premiums will always be subject to the short-term rates. The only way an option investment by itself would ever be long-term is if you purchased or sold a LEAPS option and held it for more than one year.

- **Options used in covered writes are taxed as separate securities from the underlying stock unless they are exercised.** If you close your covered write position before the expiration date or the option expires worthless, the option is taxed as a separate security. This means that you are subject to capital gains tax on the difference between the premium you received for writing the call (net of commissions) and your cost basis. If the option expires worthless, your cost basis is zero, so you pay tax on the entire sales proceeds; if you close the position, your basis is the price you paid to buy the offsetting option, so your taxable gain equals the net premium you earned minus the premium you paid. (An exception to this is that any loss with respect to a *qualified* covered call, as defined below, is treated as a long-term capital loss if at the time the loss is realized, a gain on the sale or exchange of the underlying stock would be treated as long-term.)

  If the option you wrote is assigned, then the option becomes part of the stock transaction for tax purposes. For a stock held less than a year when you're assigned, taxing the option and stock together is no different from taxing them separately, since all short term gains and losses are combined when you file, anyway. But if the stock is already a long-term holding, it could make your call long-term as well. (Additional rules governing this situation are explained below.)

Example:

Buy 100 GHI at $32

Sell 1 GHI Feb 35 call at 1.75 (after commission)

Situation	Tax Consequence
The option expires worthless	Short-term taxable gain of $175 - 0 = $175
You close the call at a profit, paying $45 for the offsetting option after commission	Short-term taxable gain of $175 - 45 = $130
You close the call at a loss, paying $225 for the offsetting option after commission	Short-term taxable loss of $175 - 225 = -$50
You are assigned	Your taxable gain of $175 from the option is added to the gain of $300 on the stock for a total gain of $475

■ **Anti-straddle rule.** The anti-straddle rule is designed to prevent the mismatching of gain and loss for tax purposes. A straddle, in IRS terms, involves "offsetting positions" where one creates "substantial diminution of risk of loss" on the other. When offsetting positions exist, the rule suspends or terminates the holding period while the offset exists and prohibits a loss to be taken on one side if there is an unrecognized gain on the other. Writing in-the-money covered calls creates an offsetting position that is subject to this rule. The rule only applies, however, to options that are in the money when written and when the stock is not yet a long-term holding. In applying the rule, the IRS makes a distinction between *qualified* and *nonqualified* calls, corresponding basically to those that are only *slightly* in the money and those that are *substantially* in the money. (The full set of criteria for determining qualified and nonqualified status is given in Appendix C.)

If, when a covered call is written, the option is *nonqualified* and the stock is *not yet long term*, the holding period of the stock is eliminated entirely while the call is in place; the holding-period clock must therefore start over at zero when the call is closed. If a covered call option is *qualified*, then the holding period of the stock is *suspended* while the call is in place; in other words, once the call is closed, the clock can pick up where it left off.

With these rules, the IRS is preventing investors from executing essentially *no-risk* tax strategies using call options but still allowing tax-deferral strategies when the call writer's positions are *at risk*. Thus, you can write out-of-the-money covered calls to defer taxable events on your portfolio, either to benefit from long-term capital gains rates or to push a tax liability into the next tax year.

■ **Fulfilling an assignment with newly purchased stock.** If you are assigned on a stock on which you have a substantial unrealized gain, you can elect to avoid the large tax liability by purchasing new shares of the same stock in the market to deliver against the assignment. You need to make sure your broker is aware that you are doing this so that the trade confirmation can indicate the new shares as the ones being delivered against the assignment. Naturally, additional commissions apply, and there is a tax consequence on the new shares to consider as well.

Say you write an August 45 call on 100 shares of General Motors stock that you have held for twenty years, at a very low cost basis, and are later assigned. You inform your broker that you want to buy 100 shares of GM *at the current market price*, which happens to be $46.30, and deliver those shares against your assignment instead of your twenty-year holding. You further instruct your broker to mark the confirmation for the sale of 100 shares via assignment with the remark "versus purchase of 100 shares at $46.30" and add the date. In this way, the 100 shares you buy in the market will be paired up with the sale of 100 shares via assignment for tax purposes, giving you a cost basis for the transaction of $46.30, and you still own your original shares, with the twenty-year holding period intact.

▪ **"Wash sale" rule.** The wash sale rule says that you may not take a tax loss on the sale of a security if within thirty days before or after that transaction, you purchase either the same or *substantially identical* security. Thus, if you have a loss on a stock and sell (or are assigned on) that position and you buy the stock again (whether you write calls on it or not) within thirty days, you will have to wait until you sell the new shares to take the tax loss on the earlier shares. Note that for the purposes of this rule, a deep in-the-money call that you buy after selling shares in the underlying stock could be considered a substantially identical security.

▪ **"Constructive sale" rule.** This rule addresses the situation in which a security has appreciated and the investor seeks to avoid the tax on the gain by selling a different security instead. If the second security eliminates the risk of loss and the upside gain potential of the first, then the investor is deemed to have entered into a "constructive sale." When this occurs, the investor must realize the gain that would have existed if the appreciated security were sold at its fair market value. As in the anti-straddle rule, writing deep in-the-money calls can potentially trigger this rule, although calls that are out of the money or those that are qualified do not.

PRECEPTS FOR COVERED CALL WRITERS

This chapter has introduced the real-world practice of covered writing. The following precepts will help you implement the strategy successfully:

▪ Don't believe you can consistently guess whether or not it is beneficial to write calls.

▪ For the most part, do not write calls on a stock if you aren't completely willing to sell it at the strike price.

■ Never forget that a covered writer is a stockholder and that the stock, rather than the option, holds virtually all the risk in the position.

■ Avoid getting so emotionally attached to any stock that you cannot bring yourself to sell it.

■ Don't buy back or roll an option simply because a rise in the underlying stock pushes it into the money. If there is time value in the option, it will almost never be assigned.

■ Don't put on a covered write simply because the option premium is compelling. Do your homework on the underlying stock first.

■ If you use a broker, pick one who is knowledgeable about options. If trading online, try to get real-time quotes.

■ Steer clear of options that trade only a few contracts a day or where there is more than a 0.30 to 0.40 point spread between the bid and the offer. If you still want to sell such calls, use a limit order, and be patient.

■ Write calls in the nearest expiration month you are comfortable with, but don't write for a premium much lower than 0.50 unless you pay very low commissions.

■ Try to write out-of-the-money strike prices to take advantage of the long-term upward bias of the stock market.

Advanced Implementations 8

High volatility is like putting your head in the oven and your feet in the refrigerator.

HARRY MARKOWITZ, 1990 Nobel Prize winner in Economics

PREVIOUS CHAPTERS HAVE EXPLORED THE BASIC CONCEPTS AND techniques any investor needs to begin a covered call program. This chapter turns to more sophisticated implementations, including the use of margin, employing underlying securities other than stocks, partial and ratio writing, and determining when an option is fairly, under-, or overvalued. These techniques are generally most appropriate for more experienced investors and professional traders. However, even a novice call writer may want to read on, to get a full flavor of the strategy's flexibility and how it can be fine-tuned to suit your particular goals and level of risk-tolerance and expertise.

COVERED WRITING ON MARGIN

Buying stocks on margin enables you to increase your investment with money borrowed from your broker. This increase in your portfolio gives you additional *leverage*, which means you earn more when your investments gain but also lose more when they decline. The aim, of course, is to earn more on the incremental investment than you spend on the interest charged to borrow the money.

With low interest rates (say, 6 percent margin), you only need to identify covered writes that return more than 0.5 percent a month to come out ahead of a straightforward cash-only investment. This sounds easy, but bear in mind that margined portfolios decline faster than cash portfolios in a bear market. Their fall is exacerbated by the fact that margin calls force you to liquidate parts of the portfolio as prices drop. When many investors who have traded on margin are forced to do this, it helps accelerate market declines.

Margin Rules for Covered Writes

Since stock is the primary investment vehicle in covered writing, margining those stocks will give the covered writer a similar leverage enhancement, but with a distinct advantage over a stock owner: The option premium received from the covered write helps meet the margin requirement. *The general initial margin requirement on a covered write when the option is out of the money is 50 percent of the stock price, less the option premium received (net of commissions).* Thus, the more premium you take in for a margined covered write, the less money you have to put up to carry the stock, and the greater your leverage.

Taken to the extreme, it would even be possible to purchase a low-priced stock on margin and identify an in-the-money call option that, when written, would supply enough premium to pay for the entire 50 percent requirement to own the stock. But the brokerage industry does not want clients purchasing stock completely with borrowed capital, so it adopted an additional rule to limit the amount that can be borrowed on in-the-money covered writes. This rule states: *When a covered write is in the money, the margin "release" (the amount they will loan you) is 50 percent of the stock price or of the strike price, whichever is lower.* The intent of this rule is not to discourage margining in-the-money covered writes but to prevent them from being initiated completely with borrowed money. Even with this rule, you can still gain quite a bit of leverage by margining in-the-money writes. Also, you can frequently find out-of-the-money options in the more distant expiration months (particularly among LEAPS) that provide enough premium to reduce the net outlay for the covered write to a fraction of the stock's cost. And these do not fall under the purview of the above margin limit.

To illustrate the leverage that margining gives a covered writer, figure 8-1 lists the potential returns of the following out-of-the-money covered write, implemented both with and without margin:

Buy 500 ZZZ at $11
Sell 5 Oct 12.5 calls at 0.75
41 days till expiration
Margin rate = 7%
Commissions excluded

Figure 8-1   Comparison of Cash and Margined Covered Writes

	Cash Covered Write	Margined Covered Write†
Net Investment	$5,125	$2,375
Return* if Unchanged	7.3%	14.9%
Return* if Exercised	21.9%	46.5%

*Returns are calculated using the net debit method. †The maximum margin of 50% is used.
Source: McMillan Analysis Corp.

Note that the covered write on 50 percent margin increases the potential returns from this position not just by a factor of two, as you might expect , but by a slightly higher factor (46.5 percent versus 21.9 percent). The reason is that the investment required in the margin scenario is not 50 percent of the cash investment, but only 46 percent: The margin requirement is 50 percent of the cost of the shares ($5,500), or $2,750, less the premium received ($375); that comes to $2,375, or 46.1 percent of the cash investment of $5,125. As you sell calls with greater premiums relative to the stock price, this effect becomes more pronounced. The more option premium a covered writer receives, the greater the leverage when buying the underlying stock on margin. *Because of this, covered writers can obtain even more leverage from margin purchases than stock buyers can.*

An in-the-money example would show a similar effect, although your margin requirement, before being reduced by the call premium, may be slightly more than 50 percent of the stock price, because of the rule mentioned. If you were to write the October call with a strike price of 10 instead of the 12.5 in the example above, the maximum your broker would lend you would be half the strike price rather than half the stock price—$2,500 instead of $2,750. Your net requirement, after subtracting the premium, would therefore be $2,625 instead of $2,375, or 51.2 percent of the cash investment. Writing in-the-money calls on margin can thus provide both attractive downside protection *and* attractive returns as a result of the leverage.

Advantages of a Margined Covered Write

The cash brought in from option premiums on the covered calls you write not only reduces your margin balance but also increases the equity in your account. This reduces your margin interest and helps cushion the account against the necessity of liquidating to meet a margin call should prices decline. Moreover, you can sometimes meet—or at least partially meet—a margin call by writing covered call options in the account rather than depositing additional cash.

Alternatively, the option premium you receive can allow you to purchase even more stock. In fact, a covered writer can sometimes acquire considerably more shares by using margin than a stock buyer can. That's because when you write calls in a margin account, the premiums you receive increase your buying power *by twice their value*. So, by using margin, you can acquire up to twice as much stock as you have capital for, write options on that position, and use the cash from the options to buy even more stock. You can then possibly write even more calls. The leverage can be substantial.

Figure 8-2 uses the following situation to illustrate how many more shares margin allows a covered writer to purchase than a buyer of the same stock.

In the margin scenario, the covered writer's capital requirement per 100 shares is half the cost of the stock (or $550) less the option premium ($175). That means the net requirement is $375 per 100 shares, excluding commissions. With $5,500, the covered writer is thus able to purchase 1,400 shares of stock ($5,500 divided by $375, times 100, rounded down to the nearest 100 shares). Margined covered writes with this much leverage are not uncommon.

Example:
ZZZ stock = $11/share
Out-of-the-money call on ZZZ = 1.75
Available funds =$5,500
Round lots only
Commissions excluded

Figure 8-2   Maximum Shares That Can Be Bought in Cash versus Margin Accounts

Stock Owner		Covered Writer	
Cash	Margin	Cash	Margin
500 shares	1,000 shares	500 shares	1,400 shares

The example above illustrates the additional advantages that covered writers with fully margined positions have over straight stock owners. The effects are even more pronounced in this example because the stock is relatively low priced. These advantages, however, do not mean that you should necessarily leverage yourself to the maximum or always use low-priced stocks. Using margin doesn't have to entail taking a more aggressive stance. Margined purchases can be used for reasonably conservative strategies, such as helping to diversify a portfolio or enabling a smaller investor to buy more stable, higher-priced stocks.

COVERED WRITING AGAINST SECURITIES OTHER THAN STOCK

Covered Writing on "Diamonds," "Qs," and Other ETFs

A host of indexes—including the Dow Jones Industrial Average (DJX), the Standard & Poor's 100 (OEX), and the Standard & Poor's 500 (SPX)—have listed options. Theoretically, you could construct a portfolio consisting of all the stocks in an index in the correct proportions in order to write index calls against it, but it would be quite impractical for an individual investor. To accommodate investors who want to use indexes in their portfolios, a number of financial institutions have created securities that track the indexes' performance but trade in shares like stock. These are called exchange-traded funds (ETFs), and some have options listed on them.

ETFs came into existence in the early 1990s with the introduction of SPDRs (Standard and Poor's Depositary Receipts) by the American Stock Exchange. They now number more than 100, including an array of funds and trusts made up of stocks or bonds grouped together for specific investment purposes. For example, there are ETFs on well-known indexes such as the Dow Jones Industrials and Russell 2000, on industry sectors such as energy and health care, and on specific countries such as Australia and Japan. Among the non-equity-based ETFs are several containing Treasury bonds of specific durations. The funds are issued by a number of prominent financial institutions, many of which identify their ETF families by brand name. For example, *Vipers* are issued by Vanguard, *iShares* by Barclays Global Investors, and *HOLDRs* by Merrill Lynch. For education or current information on ETFs, an excellent source is the American Exchange web site at www.amex.com.

Two of the most popular ETFs are Diamonds (DIA), which track the Dow Jones Industrials, and Qs (QQQ), which are shares of Nasdaq-100 Index Tracking Stock. Listed calls exist for both Diamonds and Qs. Writing calls on these securities is exactly the same as writing calls on individual stocks. For investors who seek greater diversification in their equity portfolios or who want a broad market return without the volatility of individual stocks, covered writing on ETFs could be an advantageous approach. The substantial number of strike prices on both Diamonds and Qs provide you with a high degree of flexibility in implementing the strategy.

Writing Calls against Convertible Securities

The standard terms of an equity option stipulate shares of the underlying stock as the deliverable item if assigned. Thus far, only calls covered by the underlying shares themselves have been discussed, but an equity option may be *covered* by an item other than shares of the underlying stock, *if that item is readily convertible into those shares.* That means you can write covered calls on warrants, convertible bonds, preferred stocks, or even other options, subject to certain qualifications.

The first qualification is that your convertible security must convert into *at least enough shares* to cover your short call options. If, for example, you have a bond that is convertible into 25 shares of common stock, then you would need 4 bonds to cover 1 call option. The next qualification is that the convertible security cannot mature or expire before the option's expiration date. In addition, if it has a specified conversion price into common shares—for example, a warrant for XYZ shares at $15—the strike price of the call you are writing must be the same or higher. These qualifications must be met for your brokerage to consider the convertible valid as coverage for the short call. If you have any doubts about whether a particular security qualifies, ask your broker.

Writing calls against warrants or convertible bonds is not very common, since not many such issues are available. Also, it is more challenging to find these situations, because these instruments do not show up in most of the software used to find covered writes. But if you do come across one, you can use the calculators described in Chapter 9 to figure your projected returns, and you may find them attractive.

Bear in mind, however, that convertible securities have special characteristics you need to consider when using them in your covered writing program. Some convertible bonds, for example, are callable, meaning that they can be redeemed before maturity on specified dates at specified prices. That could have significant implications for pricing (the bond might not rise above the price of its call provision) and could present a problem if your bond is called while you still have a covered write associated with it. Also, securities like convertible bonds and preferreds may have long lives or pay interest, causing them to carry significant time value over their conversion value. In that case, it will not be to your advantage to convert if you are assigned on your short call, since you would give that time value up. You would be better served by purchasing common shares to fulfill your assignment and then either holding the convertible or selling it.

Writing Calls against Other Options—The "Call-on-Call" Covered Write

Covering calls with other options is much more popular than writing against convertible bonds or preferred stocks and can be accomplished using options listed on more than 2,300 equities. These positions are not called covered writes, however. In options lingo, they're referred to as *bull calendar call spreads* or *diagonal spreads*. We prefer the term *call-on-call covered write*. However you label them, they work the same way as covered writes on stocks.

Typically, you would look for an in-the-money call to buy instead of stock. (Remember, the deeper in-the-money the call, the less time premium, and you want to minimize time premium, since it represents a cost to you in this strategy.) You need to select a call in an expiration month that is farther out than the expiration of the call you want to sell and with a strike price that is the same or lower. Otherwise, your brokerage firm will consider your short position uncovered.

The primary advantage of using an option as your underlying security rather than buying the stock is that you put up a lot less money. If you want to write a covered call on IBM when it is selling at more than $80 a share, you have to pay more than $8,000 for one round lot of the stock. Even on margin, you would need to put up $4,000 (and pay interest). If, instead, you buy a five- or six-month call option on IBM that is around 15 points in the money, your investment would probably be well under $2,000.

Your capital requirement in this case is governed by spread rules, which say that you must put up the difference between the option you purchase and the one you sell—that is, the net debit of the two positions. Essentially, that means that your long option is not marginable and must be paid for in full. To invest in spreads, you will need to be approved for the strategy by your brokerage firm and will be subject to a minimum equity requirement in your account (over and above the cost of the spread), probably equal to $10,000 or more.

Figure 8-3 shows your potential returns from writing a call against an unmargined stock position, a margined stock position, and another option, given the following situation:

Buy 100 IBM at $81.80
OR Buy 1 IBM Jan 65 call at 18.90 (149 days to expiration)
Sell 1 IBM Oct 80 call at 5.40 (58 days to expiration)
Margin rate = 7%, and margin requirement = 50% of strike price
   ($4,000)
Assume no dividend in this time period
Commissions excluded

Figure 8-3   Covered Write against Stock and against Another Option

	Covered Write on Stock (Cash)	Covered Write on Stock (Margin)	Call-on-Call Covered Write
Net Investment	$7,640	$3,640	$1,350
Return if Unchanged	4.7 %	8.7 %	20.7%*

*Assumes that the Jan 65 call will be worth 18.10 at October's expiration.
Source: McMillan Analysis Corp. Returns calculated using the net debit method.

If you choose to write against the January call, when the October expiration comes around (or anytime before, for that matter), you can roll the October call or close the whole position, just as you could if you were writing against shares. You could write calls expiring in October, November, December, or even January while continuing to use the January call to cover them (as long as you are writing a 65 or higher strike price). The amount of time premium you are paying for the January call with the stock at its current price is only 2.1 ($210). This is the cost (if held all the way to January) of using a call option instead of buying the stock at this price. Just for comparison, the margin interest on $4,180, the maximum margin release in this situation, at 7 percent for 149 days would be $119.44.

Additional considerations apply when doing call-on-call covered writing. If you are assigned on your short position, you generally will want to sell your long option, as opposed to exercising it, if it has any time value remaining. To prevent being forced to take either action, investors who write calls against other calls are usually more attentive to the short side of their position, with an eye toward rolling or closing rather than waiting for an assignment. And remember that when you cover with a call option instead of a stock, you don't receive any cash dividends, should there be any, or have any voting rights.

It might seem riskier to write a call against an option than against a stock. Actually, the reverse is often true. Granted, if you take a much larger position because it costs you less to put on, your overall risk in absolute dollars would indeed be greater. But if you buy the same position and just put less money into it, your total downside risk on that position is lower, for the same potential dollar profit. That's because a call-on-call writer has less total capital at risk than the holder of an equivalent number of shares. If IBM in the example dropped to $50, the stock owner would be down $3,180 on 100 shares, whereas the call-on-call writer would be out only the initial investment of $1,350.

When you use an option as a covering security, the time value in the long call position is an added cost, because it will decay to zero by expiration. But you can still expect to lose less money than the covered writer with stock if the stock declines in the near term. A long position in the stock declines dollar for dollar with the share price, but the long in-the-money call position loses less than a dollar for every dollar drop in the stock. That's because the option picks up more time value as its strike price gets closer to the current price of the stock. (See figure 5-3 in Chapter 5.)

To see how this works, assume that IBM in the example above suddenly dropped to $70. The covered writer who owns the stock (whether in cash or on margin) would have an unrealized loss of $11.80 per share on the holding. The call-on-call writer would lose less. An approximate theoretical value for the Jan 65 call a month into the period with IBM at $70 would be around 10, which puts the unrealized loss in the call at only 8.90. Although the option would lose as much as the stock if the share price was $70 at expiration, a call-on-call writer who closes out the position a month from now would lose less than a writer against the stock.

Covered Writing on LEAPS

As explained in Chapter 2, long-term equity anticipation securities, or LEAPS, are equity options that are issued for long periods (one, two, or three years) and that always expire in January. (LEAPS on ETFs and on indexes expire in December.) LEAPS are currently listed on about 300 stocks. For the most part, they are available on large-cap stocks with actively traded regular options. Fewer strike prices are available on LEAPS than on short-term options, and their trading volume is usually lighter.

Since LEAPS are identical to regular options except for their longer expirations, they can be used interchangeably or in conjunction with other options to create various strategies. You can write a LEAPS option against a stock as a long-term covered write, or you can use the LEAPS option as a surrogate for owning the stock (as in call-on-call writing) and write a covered call against it.

Writing a LEAPS option against stock brings in a substantial amount of option premium, which in turn lowers your investment and provides leverage. If you write a one-year LEAPS option against a stock, you have the whole year to compound your returns from that premium. What's more important, the premium you bring in can offset a substantial portion of your initial outlay for the stock. The premium received from writing an at- or slightly out-of-the-money LEAPS option against a relatively low-priced stock, for example, is often sufficient to cover nearly half the cost of purchasing the underlying stock on margin. In early 2003, for example, with Dell Computer Corp. stock trading at $27.85, a Jan '05 LEAPS option (with two years until expiration) at a strike of 30 could be sold for $6.50. The initial investment in the stock at maximum margin would be just under $1,400 for a single round lot, and the LEAPS premium of $650 would lower that to less than $750, excluding commissions. While the leverage is tempting, however, covered writers should consider the various scenarios that could unfold over a two-year period and the impact they would have on such a position.

The more popular use for a LEAPS option in a covered write is as a substitute for the underlying stock. This works exactly the same way as writing on any other call option. The strategy is thus an implementation of call-on-call writing with a longer-term option as the covering position. Since you pay more in time value for a LEAPS option, what is its advantage over a shorter-term call? For one thing, the time value in the LEAPS option declines more slowly. For another, if you hold the LEAPS option for more than one year (and do not write calls against it that will affect your holding period, as described in Chapter 7), your gains, if any, could be taxed at long-term rates. In addition, since LEAPS options tend to be more sensitive to interest rates and volatility, at a time when both of these factors are low, a LEAPS call might represent an attractive long-term purchase.

You need to be aware, however, of several differences that exist between LEAPS and regular equity options. The decay in their time value, for instance, exhibits slightly different characteristics, such as accelerating when they have only six months to expiration. Also, an at-the-money LEAPS option might not gain much value even for a sharp upward move in its underlying stock. Consequently, it is conceivable that the gain on a LEAPS option would be less than the loss on a short-term option you write against it, thereby losing you money for the period, even though your stock went up.

For more information on LEAPS, see the works listed in the bibliography, in particular McMillan's other book, *Options as a Strategic Investment*, and the CBOE website (www.cboe.com), which has information on LEAPS, including symbols and strategy discussions.

PARTIAL WRITING, MIXED WRITING, AND RATIO WRITING

Discussions thus far have assumed a one-to-one relationship between stock owned and calls written. They have also assumed that all calls written on one stock are from the same series (same month and strike price). More advanced strategies exist that involve writing more or fewer than 1 call per 100 shares of stock or writing calls in different series. Generally speaking, these strategies apply to larger portfolios, where thousands of shares of stock are involved, though they can be implemented with even a few hundred shares. In smaller portfolios, the added complexity and commissions could negate the benefits gained.

Partial Writing

Partial writing is a conservative mode of implementing an incremental return strategy. You might employ it if you hold at least 600 shares of a particular stock and want some incremental return from option premiums but don't want to have shares called away until the price rises much higher. You would start by writing calls on part of your position at a price *lower* than your ultimate target with the intention of rolling the position up (and possibly out) if the stock rises above the initial strike price. By writing on only part of the position, you are taking in incremental option income while building in "room" to roll for a credit if the stock reaches the initial strike price. That is, writing against only a fraction of your shares to begin with gives you the ability to roll not only up to a higher strike price or out to a more distant expiration but also to a position that consists of more contracts and still be fully covered.

You may not need that room, but it gives you the confidence that even if the stock moves up sharply, you will be able to roll without getting assigned at too low a strike price and without having to put in any additional money. Since you are assured that you will not be called away until your ultimate target price is reached, whatever you get from all the call writing is purely incremental.

You have to do some calculations and consider some "what-ifs" to figure out how best to implement a partial writing strategy, and you will not be able to make it work for a target price that is too high. Effective implementation may depend on how far above the strike price the stock goes before you roll.

Say you own 1,500 shares of LMN, which is trading at $56. You do not want to sell at less than $70, but no 70 strike price is yet available, or if one is, it has too little premium. You begin by writing 4 calls at the 60 strike in a relatively near month. If they expire worthless, you can write the same strike again for the next month. If the stock moves up to between $60 and $65 after you've written your calls, you could roll to the 65 strike. To insure you receive a credit, you could write up to 8 of these calls. (That way, even if the premium is half that of the 60 strike, you can still roll without putting in any additional money.) You can also move out to a more distant month. If the stock moves beyond $65 to near $70, you might roll up to the 70 strike. You could now sell up to 15 calls at the 70 strike with the confidence that you would receive at least $70 for your stock if assigned. Plus, you keep all the option premiums you accumulated along the way.

This strategy requires that you monitor your positions and roll your options accordingly. You will probably also want to recalculate the size of your call position as the stock moves or as your target price changes.

Mixed Writing

Mixed writing simply involves dividing your covered calls between two or more strike prices, expiration months, or both on the same stock. It is yet another example of the versatility of covered writing and a way to tailor the strategy to your specific needs. By writing calls with different strike prices, you can "split the difference" to fine-tune your break-even point or ultimate target price for the stock. Allocating calls between two or more expiration months can also enable you to distribute premium income more effectively throughout the year. This is particularly useful when you have an abnormally large position in a particular stock.

Say you purchase 600 shares DEF at $45 a share in January when the February 45 calls on DEF are selling at 2.50 and the February 50 calls at 1.15. You may feel that writing the 45 strike calls leaves too little upside in the stock, while the 50 strike calls offers too little premium. To produce a risk/return you are more comfortable with, you decide to write 3 contracts of each option against your long position in the stock. Figure 8-4 compares the results for the two individual writes with those for the mixed write.

If you mix covered calls with expirations in different months, the analysis becomes a bit more complicated, but the concept is the same. You're either fine-tuning your upside potential between two (or more) strike prices for a given month, or you are hedging your position between two (or more) time periods. The important point is that with mixed writing, you have even more flexibility than with single strike prices and expiration months.

Figure 8-4   Returns from Mixed Call Writing

Buy 600 DEF at $45 and Sell:	Net Investment (Break-Even Price)	Return if Unchanged*	Return if Exercised*
6 DEF Feb 45 calls at 2.50	$25,500	5.6%	5.6%
6 DEF Feb 50 calls at 1.15	$26,310	2.6%	13.7%
3 DEF Feb 45 calls plus 3 DEF Feb 50 calls	$25,905	4.1%	9.6%

*Returns are calculated on the stock investment of $27,000 and exclude commissions.

The technique of spreading your covered calls over different expiration months is applicable not only to individual stocks but to an entire portfolio as well. You might sell one- or two-month options against one-third of your portfolio, three- or four-month calls against another third, and still longer-term calls against the final third. The rationale for this would be to spread the call writing over the calendar year to insure that you are not writing them on an entire portfolio at a time when market volatility and/or prices are low.

Ratio Writing

Aggressive call writers who believe a stock will remain within a defined price range or perhaps even decline will sometimes write more than one call per 100 shares of stock held. This practice, called *ratio writing*, adds an open-ended risk component to the basic covered writing strategy, since the additional calls are naked.

Ratio writers might sell 1.5 or 2 times as many calls as they have round lots of a particular stock—writing 9 or 12 calls, for example, against 600 shares owned. The rationale is that if the stock remains flat or declines, the writer pockets that much more premium than on a simple covered write. This provides more downside protection, but at the expense of a new risk on the upside. Should the stock rise beyond the strike price (assuming for the moment that all of the calls are at the same strike), the writer makes the maximum gain on the covered part of the position and would have the stock called away. But the additional short calls must be bought back, possibly at a loss. The writer would first give back profit made on the covered write and then premium earned from the sale of the additional calls before starting to lose money overall. But the risk on the upside is still theoretically open-ended. In addition, the uncovered calls would require margin, which reduces the buying power of the account.

Figure 8-5 shows the risk-reward profile of a 2:1 ratio write compared with that of a regular covered write. The inverted V of the ratio write's profile, which shows how the strategy offers profit both above and below the strike price of the options, can be designed to coincide with a standard probability distribution curve for a given stock. In fact, as will be discussed in Chapter 9, you can calculate the probability of a stock being inside the profit range of any ratio write, given its projected volatility.

If you like the concept of a ratio write but are uncomfortable with the open-ended risk on the upside, you can cap the risk by buying calls with higher strike prices than the ones you have written in sufficient quantity to cover those that are naked. In other words, you create a credit spread on the naked calls. Of course, this adds to the cost of the strategy, reducing profits all along the profit curve. Say, in

Figure 8-5 Risk/Reward for 2:1 Ratio Write

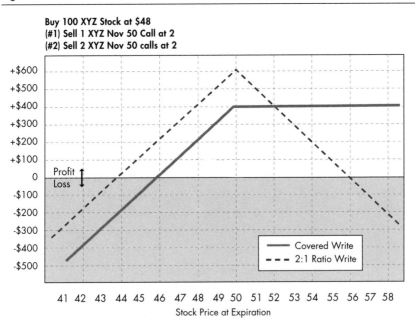

Buy 100 XYZ Stock at $48
(#1) Sell 1 XYZ Nov 50 Call at 2
(#2) Sell 2 XYZ Nov 50 calls at 2

Covered Write
2:1 Ratio Write

Stock Price at Expiration

the example in figure 8-5, you bought one XYZ Nov 55 call at 0.75. Your maximum profit on the position drops to $525 from $600. But the unlimited potential risk is removed. The worst case *on the upside* now leaves a profit of $25 before transaction costs for all prices above $55 on the stock. This does not alter the downside risk of the underlying stock position, although it does lessen both the maximum gain and the protection provided by the original ratio write by the amount paid for the long calls.

This discussion has strayed somewhat from basic covered writing. But it illustrates the flexibility one has to go beyond the normal one-to-one covered write. Before implementing such strategies, always bear in mind that adding naked options or spreads to covered writes adds to transaction costs and margin requirements. In addition, you will need to be approved by your brokerage firm for such strategies.

PUT WRITING

Strategically, selling put options is an alternative to covered call writing, since it has virtually identical risk/reward characteristics. The risk/reward graphs of the two are identically shaped, and both strategies make a limited amount of money on the upside while incurring the downside risk associated with owning stock.

A put writer is obligated to purchase the underlying stock at the strike price if the option holder exercises. Say you write the June 20 put on ABC stock when it is trading at $22, earning 2 points in premium. You are now obligated to buy the stock at $20 if assigned, but the 2 points you have received from the put sale make your actual cost basis on the stock $18, excluding commissions. That means you make a profit for all prices above $18 at expiration. Put writing is therefore a neutral-to-bullish strategy, just like covered call writing.

When writing put options, you do not need to *cover* the option with a stock position to prevent an unlimited risk. That's because the open risk of a naked put is on the *downside* and is no greater than the risk of owning stock or writing a covered call. If you are assigned, you simply buy the stock and incur the normal downside risk of owning it. You *can* cover a put option by shorting stock or by buying another put option and creating a spread, but those are different strategies. The point here is that naked put writing is very similar to covered call writing.

Advantages of Put Writing

The biggest advantage put writers have over covered call writers is that they put up much less money. When writing puts, you are required to set aside margin, either as cash or the margin value of other securities. The margin requirement for a naked put is 20 percent of the stock price, less the amount by which the put is out of the money, plus the put premium, subject to a minimum of 10 percent of the stock price. (The premium taken in can be applied against this requirement, or it can be put in a money market fund to earn interest.) That's a much smaller outlay than you would make in buying a stock for a covered write, even when the purchase is fully margined. Plus, there is no margin interest involved. Also, put writing involves only one trade execution instead of the two required in covered call writing. That means less commission and only one bid-ask spread to deal with.

Taking the same example presented in the preceding discussion, by writing the put at the 20 strike with ABC at $22, you are essentially saying that you are willing to buy the stock at a net price of $18 if it pulls back. You are also saying that if it doesn't pull back by expiration, you'll be happy to pocket 2 points for your trouble without ever having to own the stock. As a put writer, you collect premium, tying up reasonably little money or simply using the margin power of your existing portfolio, and will have to buy stock only if the price goes down. If the stock does decline, you can roll or close your position before being assigned, just as the covered call writer can. (Since naked puts are a single-security strategy, closing a position entirely, even at a small loss, is easier than with covered call writing and, as has been noted, involves lower commissions.) Or you can simply wait to be assigned, buy the stock, and then perhaps write calls against it.

Strategically, put writing fits certain situations better than covered call writing. Say there is a stock that you would like to own but that has already seen a run-up in price. You might be concerned that it is too highly valued to serve as the underlying in a covered write. In that case, you should consider selling a put option on it instead. That way, you make money if the stock continues to rise, and you buy it only if it pulls back to a more reasonable price—the strike price of the put. A major disadvantage of this approach is that if the stock has fallen substantially below the strike when it is put to you, you might not be very happy owning it. Of course, you would suffer the same disappointment in a covered write. With puts, the *biggest* disappointments occur when the underlying stock goes way up, and the most you make is the premium you received from selling the option.

Disadvantages of Put Writing

Put writing is a naked option strategy, so the requirements from your broker will involve a higher-level option approval and greater minimum account equity, perhaps on the order of $25,000. Put options also carry slightly less premium than equivalent calls (those having the same strike price and expiration) and can be slightly less liquid. And since you do not own the stock (unless assigned), you will not receive dividends. Remember as well that if you are assigned, you will need to have the capital or the margin power to carry the stock position, which will be greater than the 20 percent required to carry the naked puts themselves.

Because of the leverage involved in selling puts and the fact that you can implement the strategy with no cash or margin debit (it uses margin but does not create a debit balance), it is easier to overextend yourself with put writing than with covered call writing. Brokerage houses are aware of this, which is why they impose additional limits in the form of margin requirements or minimum account equity. You therefore need to maintain a sound perspective on the size of the positions and the type of stocks on which you write puts.

IMPLIED VOLATILITY AND OVERVALUATIONS

Shopping around for a better price or a better value is a way of life for Americans. And the search for good buys applies to investments as well as to computers or automobiles. Stock market commentators and research analysts frequently tell us that a stock is undervalued in terms of its earnings multiple, asset value, product pipeline, or a number of other measures. Options, too, can be considered cheap or expensive relative to a benchmark. As discussed in Chapter 2, the most widely used benchmark in the option industry is the Black-Scholes formula.

This formula calculates a theoretical value for any equity option from its strike price, expiration, interest rates, and the underlying stock's price and volatility. In reality, the market may price an option higher or lower than its theoretical Black-Scholes value, even after taking into account the slightly different calculations that result from using volatilities computed over different time periods. Does this mean Black-Scholes is flawed? Not really. It means that since every variable in the formula except for volatility is precisely known, the volatility being used by the market in pricing a particular option is different from the one being plugged into the equation. In other words, the market price of the option is *forecasting* a volatility for the stock during the period of the option that is different from its historical volatility. This forecast, which may be deduced from the price of the option, is called the *implied volatility*.

For example, in late 2002, Amazon shares closed at $20.30. The February 20 call (with 57 days until expiration) had a theoretical value of 1.25, based on the stock's 30-day volatility of 34 percent. But the market price of the option was 2.40, implying a volatility of 70 percent. The high implied volatility number might be due in part to the fact that the stock had declined about 10 percent on news that Christmas was slow for retailers. Whatever the reason, the options were predicting that Amazon's share price would be twice as volatile in the subsequent 60 days as it had been in the past 30. Whether this prediction would turn out to be right was another story.

Efficiency, Inefficiency, and Overvaluation

Which makes the better covered write: the May 30 call on ABC stock selling at 1.75 when the shares are trading at $30, or the May 30 call on DEF stock selling at 3.5 with the shares at $30? The answer is: You cannot tell from the information given. Certainly, DEF has the greater potential return if exercised and if unchanged. But it should also have the greater downside risk, since the price implies higher volatility and, theoretically at least, volatility is directionless. You also don't know which, if either, of these options is overvalued.

In a perfect world, the implied volatility of the two options above would be a true representation of the stock's future movements, meaning the options would be perfectly priced to account for the difference in the underlying volatilities, and the *expected returns* of the two covered writes would be equal. (Expected return is the average return one could theoretically expect if this action were repeated a large number of times.)

As we all know, however, the world is not perfect, and neither is the options market. Option buyers frequently pay more than an option is theoretically worth because, even at that higher price, the contract still represents a tremendous amount of leverage. Someone who bought those Amazon February 20 calls for 2.40 might argue that if the stock goes up to $25 and they can be sold for 5 or more, the options were bargains. This logic is false. The ability to sell an option at a profit does not alter the fact that it may have been overvalued when purchased. Had the call been priced originally at 1.25 and the stock gone up to $25, a buyer would have made nearly three times the profit. Overvaluation embodies the statistical premise that over a great number of such situations, options that are priced higher than their theoretical values will turn out to be more profitable as sales than as purchases if held until expiration.

Published statistics on the effect of overvaluation in options are scarce. However, if the Black-Scholes formula is valid and option overvaluation is indeed due to the occasional willingness of buyers as a group to overpay, then writing overvalued options is advantageous over the long term. The real key, then, to finding the best covered writes is not just looking for high premiums. It is finding situations where the option is forecasting a higher volatility in the future than the stock will actually exhibit—where it is, in other words, overvalued. Overvaluation in this sense is theoretical, since the only way to determine what is overvalued is to know what the future volatility of a stock will be. In the absence of a crystal ball, how does one do that?

A comparison of any option's price with the Black-Scholes theoretical value is a start. But the first problem you run into is whether or not Black-Scholes is giving you an accurate theoretical value to begin with. Different inputs to the formula can give you substantially different outputs where volatility is concerned. And, as noted in Chapter 2, different analysts use historical volatilities from different periods, ranging from the last 30 or 50 days to the last 100 or 200. The results can vary widely, as shown in figure 8-6.

The next problem is that every available option on a stock generates an implied volatility when its price is plugged into the Black-Scholes formula. Sometimes, options with different strikes and expiration months imply vastly different volatilities. Which one best represents the overall implied volatility?

There is no standard solution to these problems among investment firms, and different approaches can be rather complex. The one presented here is that used by coauthor Lawrence McMillan, a recognized authority on options. Mr. McMillan has been using this methodology for more than ten years at McMillan Analysis Corporation, an advisory firm that specializes in option strategies. Bear in mind, however, that McMillan's approach is proprietary and may not be representative of that used by others.

McMillan searches for options that appear overvalued relative to their own history of implied volatilities and to actual historical volatilities, as opposed to the Black-Scholes theoretical price. The first step in this process is to calculate three historical volatilities (20-day, 50-day, and 100-day) for all stocks with listed options to get a sense of whether their volatility has been increasing or decreasing and by how much. Next, the firm weights each option's implied volatility according to its trading volume and its distance in or out of the money, with the heaviest weighting given those with the highest volumes and strike prices closest to the current share price. The weighted figures are averaged to arrive at a composite implied volatility for the stock, which is then compared with the composites calculated for up to the past 600 days to determine what percentage of these the current composite is greater than. A percentile rank of 95, for instance, means that the current composite implied volatility is greater than 95 percent of those calculated for the past 600 days (or as many days as the data are available for).

Figure 8-6 Examples of Implied Volatility versus Historical Volatility

Symbol	Historical Volatility			Implied Volatility	# Days	Percentile
	20-Day	50-Day	100-Day			
MERQ	91	82	85	69	599	11
MSFT	49	54	51	35	600	21
HD	63	65	52	36	599	35
ORCL	63	72	73	63	600	39
NVDA	172	136	112	99	599	65
PTR	34	33	28	59	492	91
Z	64	54	46	73	571	91
CAL	101	85	71	106	592	96

Source: McMillan Analysis Corp.

The table in figure 8-6 shows the historical and implied volatilities for a random selection of stocks in a late 2002 sample report from McMillan Analysis Corp. The implied volatility column contains the current composite figure. The # Days column indicates how many days of past volatilities the current one was compared with, and the percentile column shows its ranking.

An investor looking at the numbers in this table might infer the following:

- The options of Mercury Interactive (MERQ), Microsoft (MSFT), and Home Depot (HD) are somewhat undervalued, since their implied volatilities are lower than their 20-, 50-, and 100-day historical volatilities and lower than the majority of their previous implied volatilities.
- The implied volatility for a stock like MERQ will create higher option premiums than those of less volatile stocks. But the options may still be undervalued if they do not reflect the actual volatility of the stock.
- Options on Oracle (ORCL) look fairly valued, given its history.
- The current volatility implied by options on Nvidia (NVDA), while high, does not fully reflect the increased volatility in the stock in the last few months.
- Petrochina Co. (PTR) options appear overvalued in light of past volatility and its own history of implied volatility.

■ Continental Airlines (CAL) options appear overvalued relative to the past two years, but fairly valued given the volatility exhibited during the past twenty days.

As mentioned above, the price of any option can be used to derive an implied volatility for the underlying stock, so you can arrive at quite different figures depending on which options you use. That is why McMillan creates a weighted composite over all available options to determine the overall implied volatility of the stock. Often there is a material disparity among the options. Some may even be undervalued while others on the same stock are overvalued. This is called a *volatility skew*. It can be caused by lopsided demand for options with a certain strike price or expiration month. Sometimes an aspect of the company's business is responsible. A drug or biotech stock, for example, might have options that appear more overvalued in October than in other months because an FDA report is due early that month on a potentially important new drug.

Option spreads can be used to capitalize on such disparities. For covered writers, however, the lesson is to check a number of different options when looking for the best one to write on a given stock. And if there's a skew, try to determine the reason—whether it's news- or event-driven, for example. A look at recent media coverage of the company will generally provide clues.

It's interesting to note that on the floor of the Chicago Board Options Exchange, the designated primary market makers (DPMs) adjust their bids and offers on the options of a particular stock by adjusting their volatility assumptions. Quotes are now computerized, since there are far too many to adjust manually every time the underlying stock moves, and the computers use the Black-Scholes formula to determine where the bid and offer should be set at any point. But when a stock begins to move more than usual because of news or events, the market makers—who must always have bids and offers for the public—simply adjust the volatility assumption for a particular stock, thus raising all the bids and offers for an entire series of options with the press of one button.

Expiration Games

Anyone who uses option strategies becomes acutely aware of the importance of expirations. On the last trading day (Friday) before an expiration day, a variety of cross currents operate on both options and their underlying stocks. On top of all the normal buying and selling are activities specific to the expiring options. Sometimes these are nonevents; other times they have a visible effect on the day's trading volume and price movements.

It is impossible to predict exactly where a stock will close on the Friday before expiration. You *can*, however, get some clues from the options as to the forces that may affect the stock's price that day. Open interest is the key. If the open interest in expiring put or call options is small—that is, in the hundreds of contracts—it will put little pressure on the price of the stock in either direction. On the other hand, if thousands or tens of thousands of expiring options are in the money on Friday, there could be a heavy supply of options for sale, since most holders prefer to sell rather than exercise. The buyers of these options will primarily be the market makers on the exchange floor, since they are obligated to provide a market, and they will be looking to hedge their positions with the stock.

Say that 10,000 call options in XYZ at the 40 strike price are expiring, and the stock is trading at $40.65. Many holders of these options will be selling to close out their positions. Market makers will be buying them and exercising to get the cash value. These market makers will likely sell the stock short when they buy the call, to "lock in" the current price. Then, over the weekend, they will exercise to buy stock at the strike price, closing their entire positions. Because this process involves the market makers selling stock during the last trading day, it tends to push the stock price down toward the strike price in the final hours of trading.

Put option open interest could presage the opposite process. If the stock is trading just *below* the strike price and put open interest is large, holders will sell their puts as a closing transaction. The market makers buy the puts, then buy stock to hedge, and finally exercise the puts to sell stock and close out the whole position. The market makers are *buying stock* in this case and thus pushing the stock back up toward the strike.

The net effect, when the size of open interest in puts is close to that in calls, is a tendency to *drive the price of the stock toward the strike price when it is already close to it*. Evidence of this phenomenon was found in the study described in Chapter 5. A sample of nearly 1,000 expirations showed that stocks closed within $1 of a strike price about 40 percent of the time (exactly what a random distribution would predict), but within $0.50 of the strike price 28 percent of the time (compared with the 20 percent that a random distribution would predict).

When stocks are wavering back and forth around a strike price at expiration, both holders and writers are on edge. If you've written calls on XYZ at the 40 strike and the stock is trading between $39.75 and $40.25 on the Friday before expiration, you could well be torn between doing nothing and rolling the call to the next month to prevent being assigned. Both tactics can be valid, depending on your desire to hold the stock and rewrite as opposed to losing the stock and having cash to reinvest. The best approach is either to decide a few days earlier what your plan will be or else to simply accept whatever happens in the final trading session.

OPTION-STOCK ARBITRAGE

The inclusion of a section on option arbitrage is not intended as an endorsement of the practice by individual investors but rather as an aid in understanding the forces at work in the options marketplace. Arbitrage as it applies to equity options exploits the relationship between the price of the stock and the prices of both the put and call options at a specific strike price. Arbitrageurs can effect a *riskless* transaction by purchasing a stock and then buying a put and selling a call on it, with both options having the same strike price and expiration. This combination is called a *conversion*. (The opposite, a short stock, short put, long call position, is called a *reversal*.)

Example:

Buy IBM

Buy IBM Jan 70 put

Sell IBM Jan 70 call

Implement all three positions for a cost under $70.

Upon expiration, if IBM is above $70, the stock will be called away for $70. If the share price is below $70, the arbs can exercise the put to sell the stock at $70. In other words, regardless of where the share price ends up, the arbs can get $70 for the stock at January's expiration. Once the conversion is implemented, the profit is guaranteed, and there are no commissions, since arbitrageurs are exchange members, but there is a cost for carrying the net position. That's where interest rates affect option prices. Arbs will put on the position if the profit they can lock in is greater than the cost of carry. So when interest rates are higher, arbs must generate a higher gross profit, meaning they will either have to receive more for the call or spend less on the put relative to what they pay for the stock.

This arbitrage helps maintain a relationship between the puts and calls with the same strike price and expiration month on a given stock. If demand for the IBM January 70 calls in the example increases without an attendant rise in the stock or in the January 70 put, their price might begin to rise, providing an attractive conversion opportunity for the arbitrageurs. They will sell the calls, buy the stock, and buy the puts. That will create demand for both the stock and the puts, bringing them more into line with the appreciated calls. Naturally, other forces are at work as well, such as the spread in valuations between the 70 strike and other strikes or between the January expiration and other months. This is the reason why an increase in a call premium does not necessarily indicate that that the stock is expected to go up. By virtue of this type of arbitrage, an increase in demand for puts with a given strike will cause both the puts and calls with that strike to rise.

Many brokerage firms have employed option-stock arbitrage for years. And why not? It's risk free and uses borrowed money. What's not to like? It is highly beneficial for the option markets as well, since it tends to keep the prices of put and call options in a set, predictable relationship with that of the underlying stock, and that is helpful for the markets overall.

Tools for Covered Writers 9

Our Age of Anxiety is, in great part, the result of trying to do today's jobs with yesterday's tools.

MARSHALL McLUHAN

YOU CAN BE A COVERED OPTION WRITER WITHOUT USING ANY OF the tools that will be discussed in this chapter. Technically, you don't even need a personal computer. You can buy stocks and write calls through a knowledgeable broker who has all the right tools on his or her desk. And if you only want to write calls on occasion and your broker is option savvy, that might work just fine.

Since you are reading this book, however, you probably play a major role (or would like to) in the management of your own investments or those of others. For you, the existence of affordable aids will be key in implementing this strategy. If you're going to manage an investment portfolio worth tens or hundreds of thousands of dollars, you have plenty of incentive to do it as efficiently and effectively as you can.

Whatever you think about the Internet's practicality for business, it is superb at "crunching" large amounts of data and making those data accessible to lots of viewers. That makes it a natural venue for creating stock and options tools. Today the software and data available on the Internet can put any individual virtually on a par with—and frequently ahead of—the professional investment community. This chapter will acquaint you with some of the tools and services available to assist investors in implementing a covered writing program, concentrating on those available through the Internet. But be aware that those mentioned by name are a mere sampling of what is available. A number of vendors and brokerage firms provide high-quality, reasonably priced, or even free, tools for covered writers. Start by seeing what your broker, or a firm you might be considering using, offers and work from there.

OPTION CHAINS

As explained in Chapter 7, an option chain is a list of all the options on a particular stock. It enables you to see quickly what strikes and expiration months are available, what the prices are, how liquid the options are, and so on. To get the same information without using a chain, you would need to know the symbols for all the options and pull up quotes on them one at a time. Such a task would become cumbersome rather quickly, even if you were working with only a single stock.

If you are an online brokerage customer, you will most likely have access to basic option chains for free. You can also obtain free chains at sites such as www.cboe.com, run by the Chicago Board Options Exchange; www.Amex.com, run by the American Exchange; and www.pcquote.com, an investment-oriented site with quotes, news, and tools, supplied by HyperFeed Technologies. To access an option chain, you generally just type in the name or symbol of the stock you're interested in, and the site's software does the rest. Some services provide option chains with real-time prices; others show prices that are twenty-minute delayed or end-of-day.

At the minimum, you will generally see the options arranged by month, showing each one's symbol, strike price, latest market price, current daily volume, and open interest. In a more detailed chain, you might see the latest bid and ask price, a hypothetical value according to Black-Scholes, and the potential returns if assigned or not at expiration. Figure 9-1 shows part of an option chain from PowerOptionsPlus, an Internet-based service for covered option writers (available at www.poweropt.com by subscription). It provides all the information mentioned plus a number of extras, such as implied volatility and the probability of the stock being above the strike price at expiration.

Most option chains base their calculations on the current price of the stock. That is, of course, what you would need to determine the potential returns on all the different possible covered writes. But if you already own a stock, you would want to see the projected returns calculated on the price at which you purchased it. PowerOptionsPlus enables you to do this (as an illustration, see figure 9-2). You can also calculate returns based on a specified repurchase price for an option, in case you are closing a position early or rolling to another.

Figure 9-1   Option Chain from PowerOptionsPlus

One glance at an option chain like this shows you all the available call strikes in each month, with symbols, prices, volume, theoretical value, and more.

More Info	Call Strike	Opt. Sym.	Opt. Last	Opt. Bid	Opt. Ask	Black Sch.	Opt. Vol.	Open Int.	If Not Asgnd	If Asgnd	If Not Asgnd Annual	If Asgnd Annual	% To Dbl.	Delta	Implied Volat.	% Time Value	% Prob. Above
Dell Computer Corp. (DELL) $ 25.27							FEB	Expiring 2/22/2003 24 days left									
	15.0	DLYBC	9.40	10.20	10.40	10.29	0	574	40.4%	-0.5%	614%	-7%	40.3%	1.00	0.32	0.0%	100.0%
	17.5	DLYBW	6.90	7.80	7.90	7.79	0	495	30.9%	0.2%	469%	3%	30.9%	1.00	0.32	0.1%	99.9%
	20.0	DLYBD	5.30	5.30	5.50	5.30	0	916	21.0%	0.2%	319%	2%	21.0%	1.00	0.32	0.1%	99.7%
	22.5	DLQBX	2.70	3.00	3.10	2.87	172	3540	11.9%	1.0%	181%	16%	12.8%	0.93	0.32	0.9%	91.9%
	25.0	DLQBE	1.15	1.15	1.20	0.99	2960	27457	4.6%	3.6%	69%	55%	6.0%	0.57	0.41	3.4%	54.2%
	27.5	DLQBY	0.30	0.25	0.30	0.18	702	28170	1.0%	9.9%	15%	151%	3.7%	0.17	0.37	1.0%	18.4%
	30.0	DLQBF	0.10	0.05	0.10	0.02	420	48844	0.2%	19.0%	3%	288%	3.0%	0.02	0.39	0.2%	4.3%
	32.5	DLQBZ	0.05	-	0.05	-	11	22065	-	-	-	-	-	-	-	-	-
	35.0	DLQBG	0.05	-	0.05	-	0	13147	-	-	-	-	-	-	-	-	-
Dell Computer Corp. (DELL) $ 25.27							MAR	Expiring 3/22/2003 52 days left									
	17.5	DLYCW	-	7.80	8.00	7.81	0	0	30.9%	0.2%	217%	1%	30.9%	1.00	0.32	0.1%	99.8%
	20.0	DLYCD	4.80	5.50	5.60	5.34	1	31	21.8%	1.2%	153%	8%	22.3%	0.98	0.32	0.9%	97.2%
	22.5	DLQCX	2.75	3.40	3.50	3.08	4	331	13.5%	2.9%	94%	20%	15.3%	0.85	0.49	2.5%	73.6%
	25.0	DLQCE	1.70	1.70	1.75	1.39	146	3734	6.7%	6.1%	47%	43%	10.4%	0.57	0.41	5.6%	52.9%
	27.5	DLQCF	0.70	0.65	0.70	0.48	1025	4563	2.6%	11.7%	18%	82%	6.2%	0.27	0.39	2.6%	28.1%
	30.0	DLQCF	0.15	0.15	0.20	0.13	132	421	0.6%	19.4%	4%	136%	4.4%	0.09	0.33	0.6%	8.7%
	32.5	DLQCZ	0.10	-	0.10	-	0	400	-	-	-	-	-	-	-	-	-
Dell Computer Corp. (DELL) $ 25.27							MAY	Expiring 5/17/2003 108 days left									
	15.0	DLYEC	10.10	10.40	10.60	10.33	0	131	41.2%	0.9%	139%	3%	41.2%	1.00	0.32	0.5%	99.8%
	17.5	DLYEW	7.80	8.10	8.20	7.86	0	166	32.1%	1.9%	108%	6%	32.5%	0.99	0.32	1.3%	98.1%
	20.0	DLYED	5.20	5.90	6.00	5.51	0	303	23.3%	3.3%	79%	11%	24.1%	0.92	0.49	3.3%	81.1%
	22.5	DLQEX	3.50	4.00	4.10	3.48	4	763	15.8%	5.8%	53%	20%	19.2%	0.78	0.49	4.8%	67.0%
	25.0	DLQEE	2.45	2.45	2.55	1.95	210	10299	9.7%	9.6%	33%	32%	14.9%	0.57	0.41	8.6%	52.0%
	27.5	DLQEY	1.30	1.30	1.40	0.98	223	8314	5.1%	14.7%	17%	50%	9.9%	0.36	0.39	5.1%	34.3%
	30.0	DLQEF	0.60	0.60	0.65	0.44	46	18932	2.4%	21.6%	8%	73%	7.8%	0.19	0.37	2.4%	19.4%
	32.5	DLQEZ	0.25	0.25	0.30	0.18	127	7781	1.0%	29.9%	3%	101%	6.3%	0.09	0.35	1.0%	9.6%
	35.0	DLQEG	0.15	0.10	0.15	0.07	0	16694	0.4%	39.1%	1%	132%	5.7%	0.04	0.34	0.4%	4.1%

Source: PowerOptionsPlus

Figure 9-2   Option Chain Inputs at PowerOptionsPlus

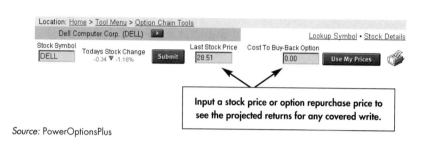

Source: PowerOptionsPlus

SEARCH TOOLS

With some 2,300 stocks and 50,000 call options available at any time, it is easy to appreciate the benefit of a search tool. Such tools consist of software applications that enable you to comb the pool of stocks and options for combinations that fit your criteria, generally also ranking

Figure 9-3   Input Screen for Search Function

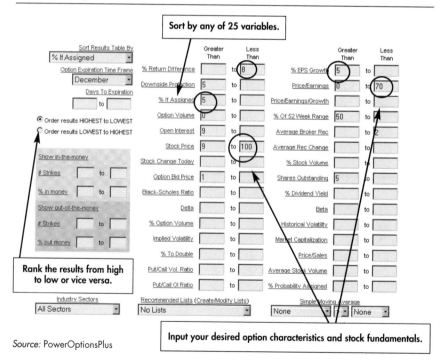

Source: PowerOptionsPlus

Figure 9-4   Search Results

| | | | | | | | | % | | | | | | Avg. | | |
Stock Sym	Last Stock Price & Chg.	Option Sym	Expire/Strike & Days To Exp.	Opt. Bid	Opt. Vol.	Open Int.	Opt. Vol.	Dnsd. Prot.	% Assnd	% Epsq	P/E	P/E/G	% Of Rnge	Rec. (#)	% Vol	Delta
TTWO	25.72 (-1.91)	TUOLE	02 DEC 25.0 (60)	3.90	115	558	129	15.2	14.6	33	19	0.57	76	1.9 (15)	100	0.60
COCO	35.58 (-3.63)	UCSLG	02 DEC 35.0 (60)	4.60	6	10	211	12.9	13.0	32	41	1.27	84	1.4 (5)	96	0.58
SPW	95.34 (-16.01)	SPWLT	02 DEC 100.0 (60)	6.50	83	221	296	6.8	12.6	45	16	0.35	57	1.4 (9)	107	0.43
PSUN	22.00 (-0.31)	PVQLX	02 DEC 22.5 (60)	2.00	9	286	51	9.1	12.5	20	22	1.11	66	1.6 (16)	49	0.51
MGG	33.29 (-1.21)	MGGLG	02 DEC 35.0 (60)	1.75	31	701	12	5.3	11.0	70	28	0.40	58	1.8 (19)	91	0.42
CHS	19.53 (-0.53)	CHSLD	02 DEC 20.0 (60)	1.50	2	10	126	7.7	10.9	16	31	1.98	89	1.8 (13)	100	0.52
ERTS	66.82 (-5.32)	EZQLN	02 DEC 70.0 (60)	3.70	92	1503	181	5.5	10.9	94	63	0.67	75	1.5 (19)	128	0.40
LEN	57.53 (-2.30)	LENLL	02 DEC 60.0 (60)	3.30	6	50	114	5.7	10.6	7	8	1.15	80	1.4 (11)	99	0.46
MIK	44.00 (-1.37)	MIKLI	02 DEC 45.0 (60)	3.30	4	487	105	7.5	10.6	19	24	1.28	74	1.3 (12)	86	0.51
PIR	19.24 (-0.99)	PIRLD	02 DEC 20.0 (60)	1.15	4	438	91	6.0	10.6	8	16	1.97	63	1.6 (11)	58	0.48
LOW	42.93 (-1.47)	LOWLI	02 DEC 45.0 (60)	2.15	142	158	414	5.0	10.3	7	26	3.53	60	1.7 (21)	86	0.46
SPW	95.34 (-16.01)	SPWLS	02 DEC 95.0 (60)	9.00	86	54	296	9.4	10.0	45	16	0.35	57	1.4 (9)	107	0.55
CAI	38.89 (+0.31)	CAILH	02 DEC 40.0 (60)	2.50	3	464	46	6.4	9.9	19	33	1.69	88	1.5 (11)	116	0.38
DP	43.38 (-0.60)	DPLI	02 DEC 45.0 (60)	2.40	10	149	177	5.5	9.8	10	28	2.86	57	1.0 (2)	278	0.38
CMX	17.30 (+0.68)	CMXLW	02 DEC 17.5 (60)	1.20	516	2280	287	6.9	8.7	16	19	1.18	54	1.4 (16)	98	0.52

Rick Lehman's Covered Call SmartSearchXL Results
Tuesday, 10/22/2002 2:33:03 PM EST - 20 minute delayed — December ordered by Assigned - Filtered

The search provides a list of covered writes that match your criteria and are ranked by return.

Source: PowerOptionsPlus

the candidates according to criteria you select as well. You can conduct open searches just to see what opportunities exist from the broad universe, or you can zero in on stocks whose fundamentals will round out or balance your portfolio. You can also specify lists, such as the Value Line or Standard & Poor's research lists, within which to search.

Services such as PowerOptionsPlus's SmartSearchXL allow you to input data ranges for option criteria as well as stock fundamentals and then sort the results by any of twenty-five variables. The screen used to select parameters is illustrated in figure 9-3; the partial results of that search are shown in figure 9-4.

CALCULATORS

A number of calculators are available to supplement what you find in an option chain or from a search. These are handy for doing "what if" analyses on different positions, enabling you to input

Figure 9-5 Covered Call Calculator

Results	Calculate		
Expiration Date 11/15/2002		**Days to Expiration** 24	

Cash Returns (No Margin Used)

Net Investment	6520		
Return if exercised	7.36 %	Return if unchanged	3.98 %
Downside Break-Even Pt.	32.6	% Downside Protection	1.17 %

Margin Returns

Net Investment

Net Investment	6503		
Return if Exercised	7.38 %	Return if Unchanged	3.99 %
Downside Break-Even Pt.	32.6	% Downside Protection	1.17 %

Source: McMillan Analysis Corp.

data that may be different from the default values used in the general search tools.

McMillan Analysis Corp. operates a website, www.optionstrategist .com, where you can access the free covered call writing calculator shown in figure 9-5, among other useful resources. When you input the data for a particular covered call, the calculator gives you returns and break-even prices for both cash and margin accounts.

PowerOptionsPlus offers subscribers a Black-Scholes calculator, shown in figure 9-6, that enables users to derive theoretical option values using their own figures for the various factors. This is particularly useful if you want to input a volatility assumption different from the one used in more general calculations.

Probability Analysis

When you're evaluating covered write candidates, potential return is important, but you may also want to know how likely you are to realize that return. That depends on the likelihood that the underlying stock will reach the strike price of a particular option. You might, for

Figure 9-6 Black-Scholes Calculator

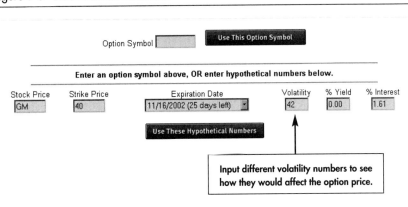

instance, see a potential covered write on a stock trading at $12 that has a listed call option two or three months out with a 30 strike price and, despite the large potential RIE, reject it because you see little chance of the shares reaching that price within that period. In making such a decision, you would consider factors such as market sentiment and business prospects. A computer program is little help in such an assessment. It *can*, however, calculate the *mathematical* probability of a stock reaching a certain price, based on its historical performance.

McMillan's Option Strategist site offers a free Simple Probability Calculator that will tell you the probability (using a standard log normal distribution formula) of a stock exceeding a given strike price at expiration, based on its historical volatility. Subscribers to the Strategy Zone section of the site, which provides analytical tools and data in support of a number of option strategies, can go a step farther using a Monte Carlo calculator. This uses scenario simulations to derive the probabilities of a stock reaching various prices in the same way that NASA simulates the probability of a part failure on a space shuttle. The Monte Carlo calculator not only generates more accurate probabilities due to its simulation methodology but can also predict the likelihood of a stock reaching target prices at any time *during* a period, rather than simply at the *end* (that is, at expiration). It is thus particularly suitable for developing "what if"

Figure 9-7   Covered Writes Ranked by Annualized Expected Return

Stock	Price	Strike & Month	Call Price	Return if Exercised
ISIS	11.25	12.5A	3.69	62.5
VXGN	9.75	10.0B	3.31	52.2
RMG	8.38	10.0L	1.88	50.8
ENDP	8.63	10.0I	0.63	22.8
CAL	8.63	10.0I	0.75	24.8
IMCL	9.25	10.0K	1.88	33.1
RFMD	8.13	15.0B	0.56	95.1
NOVN	12.88	15.0I	0.88	23.6
EAGL	10.00	12.5I	0.38	28.0
QSFT	10.00	12.5J	0.88	35.0
PMCS	8.63	10.0K	1.31	34.2
IMCL	9.25	10.0B	2.69	49.3
FFIV	14.00	15.0J	2.00	23.6
DPMI	27.00	30.0I	1.63	17.6
AEM	13.50	17.5I	0.25	30.7
ISIL	19.13	20.0I	1.94	15.4
UTSI	14.25	15.0I	1.25	14.1

Source: McMillan Analysis Corp.

scenarios and determining decision points for tactics like rolling the options in a covered write.

For subscribers, the Strategy Zone also publishes daily tables of covered writes together with associated probabilities, derived using Monte Carlo simulation. The tables display the likelihoods that the underlying stock for a particular covered write will reach the downside and upside break-even prices (the price at which the covered write begins to make money and the crossover price, above which stock alone does better than the covered write) as well as its chances of being at the strike price at expiration, thus generating the maximum gain for the covered write. The table also includes a column for "expected" return. This is derived by taking the various returns a covered write would generate at expiration under different price scenarios for the underlying stock, multiplying each return by the probability of the stock reaching the associ-

Annualized RIE	Probability of DBE	Probability of RIE	Probability of UBE	Expected Return	Annualized Expected Return
148	65	46	36	23	54.1
101	71	49	34	24	45.9
147	61	41	34	13	38.8
238	59	30	25	4	38.5
258	58	35	29	3	34.7
133	64	45	35	9	34.3
184	53	19	18	18	34.3
246	58	32	27	3	33.3
292	54	20	18	3	32.3
203	57	31	27	6	32.1
137	61	39	31	8	31.1
95	65	46	36	16	30.4
137	63	44	**34**	5	29.0
183	59	**34**	27	3	28.7
320	**52**	14	13	3	27.7
161	63	44	33	3	27.5
147	63	42	31	3	27.5

Probabilities of hitting downside break-even (DBE) price, of realizing the return if exercised (RIE), and of reaching the upside break-even (UBE) price (crossover point)

ated price, and summing the resulting products. Expected return as used here is thus the average return one could expect from a large number of repetitions of the same covered write. Figure 9-7 shows a sample table, with the covered writes ranked by annualized expected return.

CallWriter.com, a subscription-based website operated by financial products company LogiCapital Corp., offers a tool called the Position Management Calculator (pictured in figure 9-8 on the following page). This calculator was designed to help users optimize their covered writes *after* initiating them. The calculator does this by computing the potential return for follow-up actions such as rolling to different call options and comparing these with the potential return from remaining with the current position.

Figure 9-8 Position Management Calculator

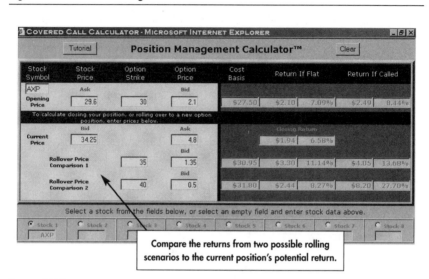

Source: CallWriter.com

INDUSTRIAL STRENGTH OPTION SOFTWARE

As noted earlier, covered writing can be as simple or as complicated as you want to make it. Many individuals, particularly those looking to write calls on stocks they already own, can implement a basic covered writing plan quite effectively using the online data provided by their brokerage firms. For those who want to go beyond covered call writing into the broader world of option strategies, however, option software even more sophisticated than that previously discussed exists. Option-Vue 5, from OptionVue Systems International (www.optionvue.com), and PowerAnalyzer, from McMillan Analysis Corp., for example, offer features such as:

- High-powered, real-time option analysis
- Multistrategy analysis
- Risk management capabilities
- Overvalue/undervalue lists and screening
- Probability analysis
- Volatility charting

Whatever tools you use, bear in mind that they simply manipulate data, make calculations, and present results. You need to perform your own *due diligence* to ascertain the accuracy of the results. A computer may, for example, pick up a bogus price quote and calculate projected returns on it. It's also up to you to evaluate what the program turns up. A computer has no idea *why* a particular covered write looks so good; it just reports things as it sees them. Call premiums on a stock can appear to offer attractive returns, for example, but the stock itself may be too risky for you. You must assess these possibilities before you invest in any stock or option position generated by computer software.

WHAT WILL THIS COST YOU?

If you are concerned about the cost of the type of tools mentioned in this chapter, you can rest easy. Most of the information discussed here is surprisingly affordable, if not free. Quotes and basic option chains are provided for free at numerous places on the Internet, some of which are listed on the following two pages. Also, most brokerages make that type of information available online to their clients at no charge. If your firm does not provide free quotes and option chains, then you will have no trouble finding one that does. In addition, several of the websites mentioned in this chapter offer additional free tools like calculators and graphs.

As for the subscription services and software products, those, of course, will vary in price. You will find, however, that a number of the subscription services are available at prices beginning in the range of $20 to $50 per month. This is a very modest cost for the benefit that can be derived from these services, even in a relatively small account. More sophisticated services and software that includes proprietary ideas and research can certainly cost more, and should be evaluated in light of the additional benefit you would receive.

We advise that covered writers avail themselves of information from multiple sources, particularly when it's free. You will probably find, as we have, that different sources have different strengths. One might be better for option chains, while another has real-time quotes, and still another has the best graphs. The cost to you for many of these services is simply the time it takes to find the ones you find helpful.

INTERNET RESOURCES FOR COVERED CALL WRITERS

URL	Organization	Description
www.amex.com	American Stock Exchange	The Amex stock exchange's website offers quotes, symbols, and option chains, as well as educational information on equities, options, EFTs (free).
www.cboe.com	Chicago Board Options Exchange	At the CBOE's site visitors can access quotes, symbols, option chains, the Options Disclosure Document, a learning center, the BuyWrite Index, calculators, and information on taxes (free).
www.optionsclearing.com	Options Clearing Corp.	The OCC, the organization primarily responsible for processing option trades, runs this site, offering visitors news, option adjustments, market statistics, and industry information (free).
www.optionscentral.com or www.888options.com	Options Industry Council	The OIC is a nonprofit association dedicated to educating investors about options. Its website includes a learning center, information on seminars and events, and a bookstore (free).

Vendors

URL	Organization	Description
www.pcquote.com	PcQuote.com	A subsidiary of HyperFeed Technologies, PcQuote.com provides quotes, news, and option chains (free and subscription).
www.poweropt.com or www.poweroptionsplus.com	PowerOptionsPlus	PowerOptionsPlus is a Web-based service that provides options calculators, search screens, option chains, and commentary on covered writing and other options strategies. Subscribers can also link directly to sites providing stock research and charts (free and subscription).
www.callwriter.com	LogiCapital Corp.	CallWriter provides daily picks, lists of covered writes in real time, and a position management calculator (subscription).

www.optionvue.com	OptionVue Systems	OptionVue Systems International is a software development firm whose primary focus is leading-edge analytical systems for trading options. The firm was founded by Len Yates, a former options trader and recognized analytic software professional (subscription).

Charting sites

www.bigcharts.com	MarketWatch.com, Inc.	BigCharts.com is an investment research website providing access to professional-level research tools such as interactive charts, quotes, industry analysis, intra-day stock screeners, and market news, historical stock prices, and commentary (free).
www.stockcharts.com	StockCharts.com, Inc.	StockCharts.com provides quotes, symbols, and option strings (free and subscription).

Authors' sites

www.coveredwriter.com	Lehman Investment Advisors	Lehman provides general and reference information on covered call writing plus an online subscription service for covered writers containing daily ideas, market commentary, and and sample portfolios (free and subscription).
www.optionstrategist.com	McMillan Analysis Corp.	McMillan Analysis Corp. provides data, reports, commentary, analysis, and tools for a variety of options strate-strategies. The site also offers online seminars, phone hotlines, and e-mail newsletter services (free and subscription).

Afterword

COVERED CALL WRITING WILL CHANGE THE WAY YOU THINK about investing. Among other things, it will change your stock selection process, your timing, your expectations, and your exit strategy. It is likely that your ability to embrace these changes, rather than the difference in returns on your holdings, will ultimately determine whether you choose to adopt covered writing as your ongoing strategy. If you do, you can derive most of its benefits with even a very basic implementation of the technique. Make no mistake, however. Covered writing is very definitely a hands-on strategy. You can write calls incrementally on one or two of your stock positions with very little effort, but if you intend to make call writing your primary investment strategy, you should be prepared to do some work each month on your portfolio.

The chapters in this book have presented covered call writing as an investment strategy, introducing its fundamental principles and the tools necessary for implementing it. This final section takes a step from theory to reality in showing how the authors actually apply the lessons presented throughout the book. Among the numerous advantages of covered writing, we tend to find the following the most attractive:

■ **The flexibility to tailor the risk/reward of any stock position and to change that risk/reward at any time.** The flexibility that call options add to stock investing is unmatched by any other investment vehicle. Individual stocks represent a huge variety of risks and opportunities. No matter what a stock is expected to do, however, there is generally a way it can be played with a covered write. The authors, for instance, write covered calls on stocks with attractive long-term potential and on ones that are expected to have major announcements in the following week. We will also write them on stocks that are running up strongly, and on ones that have tumbled.

▪ **The ability to obtain at least some profit from the passage of time, regardless of market direction.** The authors follow numerous technical indicators for clues to the market's short-term direction in the hope of capitalizing on a major move in either direction. But for much of any given year, the market may not make such a move. Covered writing works for the investor all the time, regardless of market moves.

▪ **The ability to equal or exceed overall market returns over the long term.** The studies cited in this book show that a basic covered call writing program can match the overall returns in equities over the long term. The authors' approach, however, is more aggressive, aiming not just to match but to exceed the returns in the equity markets on a regular basis. Like the mechanics who use precision engineering to coax more power out of a race car engine, we view covered call writing as a way to coax more return out of the equity markets.

▪ **The ability to play special situations with the odds in your favor.** When speculation, news, or special events cause a stock to gyrate wildly, option premiums can get highly overvalued in the short term. Such situations offer exceptional opportunities for short-term gain. We like to capitalize on these situations using covered writes. This may not yield the big win that buying the stock or a call option might, but we profit more frequently and over a wider range of outcomes.

To see how an aggressive approach to covered writing can work in the real world, consider the following one-week snapshot of the activity in the account of one of our clients. The client wants aggressive long-term growth from covered writing. At the time illustrated, the account was less than one month old and just getting initially invested. Circumstances in the market and in individual stocks, however, had already created the need to take both defensive and aggressive follow-up actions on recently initiated positions.

Portfolio: $30,000
Account type: Margin
Timing: Account initiated at the end of December 2002

The equity markets were weak during the Christmas–New Year's period. This signaled the possibility of a decline in January, so it was decided that very short-term at- or in-the-money covered writes with at least 5 percent protection were in order. The following three positions were initiated.

Date	Action	Position	Circumstances/Rationale
Jan 1	New Position	Bought 400 TXN at $15.08/share Sold 4 TXN Jan 15 calls at 0.90	The at-the-money covered write will return 5.4% in less than 3 weeks if assigned, with 6.0% downside protection.
Jan 1	New Position	Bought 200 NCEN at $25.75/share Sold 2 NCEN Jan 25 calls at 2	The in-the-money covered write will return 4.9% if assigned, with 7.8% downside protection.
Jan 1	New Position	Bought 400 QQQ at $24.86/share Sold 4 QQQ Jan 24 calls at 1.25	The in-the-money covered write will return 1.6% if assigned, with 5.0% downside protection.

Contrary to prior expectation, the beginning days of 2003 showed surprising strength in the equity markets and indications were that this strength would continue for at least a week or two. A more bullish posture was adopted.

Date	Action	Position	Circumstances/Rationale
Jan 3	New Position	Bought 200 CDWC at $44.37/share Sold 2 CDWC Jan 45 calls at 1.75	The slightly out-of-the-money covered write will return 5.4% if assigned, with 3.9% downside protection.
Jan 3	New Position	Bought 300 PPD at $26.43/share Sold 3 PPD Jan 25 calls at 2.35	The in-the-money covered write will return 3.5% if assigned, with 8.9% downside protection.

Negative news came out on PPD over the weekend of January 4-5. The stock dropped right from the open on Monday morning January 6 and traded as low as $18.39 before closing at $19.57—a decline of more than 25 percent in one day. To minimize the loss, the original calls were covered at a profit and lower ones written.

Date	Action	Position	Circumstances/Rationale
Jan 6	Roll down	Closed 3 PPD Jan 25 calls at 0.25 Sold 3 PPD Jan 20 calls at 1.10	If assigned, the covered writes on PPD will lose 12.2%, whereas at a price of $20, a stock owner will lose 24.3%. (In addition, we initiated bullish put spreads for February at the $17.5 strike price.)
Jan 7	New Position	Bought 200 BVF at $28.30/share Sold 2 BVF Jan 30 calls at 0.45	The stock appeared to have excellent long-term potential. If assigned, the covered call will return 4.0% in slightly more than one week, with 1.6% downside protection.
Jan 8	Roll up	Closed 4 QQQ Jan 24 calls at 2.05 Sold 2 QQQ Jan 25 calls at 1.25 Sold 2 QQQ Jan 26 calls at .65	QQQ had moved up substantially and was now near $26. The roll up to $25 and $26 strike prices allowed for more upside potential in the position, albeit with additional risk.

This offers a glimpse into the real-world practice of covered writing in an aggressive account. It is representative of both the opportunities and the risks involved in covered writing, as well as of the flexibility to deal with these as they occur. Options are not for everyone. Our aim is not to make covered writers out of people who are not well suited to the strategy. It is to educate and assist those who are. If you are one of them, we suggest that you do two things: Sign option papers on at least one of your brokerage accounts, and identify a covered call opportunity for your portfolio. Neither of these actions will cost you anything or obligate you in any way. They will just give you the option.

APPENDIXES

Appendix A

Timeline of Options Trading in the United States

Late   Advertisements begin to appear in newspapers for put and call
1800s options by broker-dealers who make the arrangements directly
between the buyers and sellers on a one-to-one basis.

1920s Abuses and trading scams involving both stocks and options are
perpetrated on an unsuspecting public by unscrupulous players.

1929 In the aftermath of the Crash of 1929, the Security and Exchange
Commission investigates the trading of stocks and options to
establish rules that protect the public and facilitate the legitimate
use of these instruments. A prominent put-call broker named
Herbert Filer saves options from potential demise by testifying to
the SEC on their legitimate purposes and economic value.

1934 **The Securities and Exchange Act of 1934 gives the SEC regulatory authority for options trading.**

1973 **On April 26, the Chicago Board Options Exchange (CBOE) becomes the first formal securities exchange to list stock options. On this day, trading begins with call options on sixteen U.S. stocks.**

1973 University of Chicago professors Fischer Black and Myron
Scholes write an article entitled "The Pricing of Options and Corporate Liabilities" that applies the mathematics of physical heat-transfer to a theoretical formula for determining the price of any
financial instrument with an expiration date. The Black-Scholes
formula becomes the standard by which professionals assess the
value of stock options. (In 1997 Scholes is awarded the Nobel
Prize for Economics for this formula, Black being deceased.)

1975 The options exchanges agree to adopt the CBOE's Clearing Corporation (established in 1972) as the central clearing facility and guarantor of options for the industry, renaming it the Options Clearing Corporation (OCC).

1977 Trading in put options is added on all option exchanges.

1983 Options are traded for the first time on a stock index, the CBOE 100 Index (OEX), which is later renamed the S&P 100 Index.

1990 Options having expirations of one year and longer—called long-term equity anticipation securities, or LEAPS—begin trading.

1998 The NASD merges with the AMEX and PHLX exchanges. The CBOE also merges, with the PCX exchange. (Technology-based reductions in cost plus reduced duplication in trading are the primary reasons for these mergers.)

Sample Covered Writing Spreadsheet for Tax Purposes

[A]	[B]	[C]	[D]	[E]	[F]	[G]	[H]	[I]
		CAPITAL GAINS AND LOSSES						
							Tax year	
	Name(s) from Form 1040					SS#		
Short-term Capital Gains and Losses								
	(a) Description	(b) Date	(c) Date	(d) Sale	(e) Cost			
Line #	of Property	Acquired	Sold	Price	Basis	(f) Loss	(g) Gain	
1								
2								
3								
4								
5								
6								
7								
8								
9								
10								
	TOTAL			0.00	0.00	0.00	0.00	
Long-term Capital Gains and Losses								
1								
2								
3								
4								
5								
	TOTAL			0.00	0.00	0.00	0.00	

Appendix C

Tax Rules for "Qualified" Covered Call Options

The IRS has established a set of rules to determine whether the writing of a covered call will affect the holding period of the underlying stock for tax purposes. The objective is to prevent individuals from writing deep in-the-money covered calls strictly for the purpose of deferring a taxable gain, while not penalizing writers who are using covered calls for other purposes. The assumption is that if a call is far enough in the money, the writer is primarily using the strategy for tax purposes. The crux of the rules, therefore, is to specify how much (or how deeply) in-the-money a covered call can be written before it affects the holding period of the underlying security for tax purposes.

These rules apply only to *in-the-money* calls and result in calls being either "qualified" or not, depending on how deeply in-the-money they are when first written. Holding periods of the underlying stock are affected as follows:

Type of call	Effect on Holding Period
All out-of-the-money covered calls	No effect
Qualified in-the-money calls	The holding period of the stock is *suspended* while the call is in place
Non-Qualified in-the-money calls	If the holding period of the stock is not yet long term, then it is *eliminated* entirely while the call is in place. (If the holding period is already long term, then there is no effect.)

To be qualified, a covered call must:

- be exchange-traded and written on stock held by the investor or purchased in connection with the sale of the call
- have more than 30 days to expiration and a strike price no lower than the first one available below the closing price of the stock on

203

the day before the option was written.

■ (if written more than 90 days before expiration with a strike price over $50) have a strike price no lower than the second available strike price below the closing stock price on the previous day.

■ (if written on a stock trading at $150 or less) not be more than $10 in the money.

From these rules, the following tables have been constructed.

Previous Day's Closing Stock Price*	Lowest Applicable Strike for the Option to be Considered Qualified
Stocks trading under $25 with calls having less than 30 days to expiration	None
Stocks trading under $25 with calls having more than 30 days to expiration	
$5.01–$5.88	5
$5.89–$7.50	None
$7.51–$8.82	7.5
$8.83–$10	None
$10.01–$11.76	10
$11.77–$12.50	None
$12.51–$14.70	12.5
$14.71–$15	None
$15.01–$17.64	15
$17.65–$20	17.5
$20.01–$22.50	20
$22.51–$25	22.5
Stocks trading over $25 with calls having less than 30 days to expiration	None
Stocks trading over $25 with calls having having more than 30 days to expiration	
$25.01–$60 More than 30 days to expiration	One strike below previous day's closing stock price

Previous Day's Closing Stock Price*	Lowest Applicable Strike for the Option to be Considered Qualified
Stocks trading over $25 with calls having more than 30 days to expiration (cont.)	
$60.01–$150 31–90 days to expiration	One strike below previous day's closing stock price
$60.01–$150 More than 90 days to expiration	Two strikes below previous day's closing stock price (but not more than $10 in the money)
Over $150 31–90 days to expiration	One strike below previous day's closing stock price
Over $150 More than 90 days to expiration strikes below previous day's closing stock price	Two strikes below previous day's closing stock price

*In all cases, if the opening price of the stock on the day the option is written is greater than 110 percent of the preceding day's closing price, that opening price, rather than the preceding day's closing price, is used in determining the lowest acceptable strike price for a qualified covered call.

Different strike price intervals (for example, $2.50 as opposed to $5.00) may exist for various options on comparably priced stocks. Also, stock splits may result in odd strike prices.

Additional Rules

Even if the stock/strike price rules are satisfied, a call that is not an option to purchase stock acquired by the investor in connection with the writing of the option would not be qualified. In other words, a call written on September 20, 2002, will not be qualified if the stock is purchased on September 24, 2002.

Any loss with respect to a qualified covered call is treated as a long-term capital loss if, at the time the loss is realized, a gain on the sale or exchange of the underlying stock would be treated as long-term.

When a covered call is disposed of (i.e., closed) at a loss in one tax year and the stock is still owned on the first day of the subsequent year, the stock must be held an additional 30 days from the date of disposition of the call in order for the covered call to be treated as qualified.

Similarly, a covered call is not treated as qualified if it is not held for 30 days after the related stock is disposed of as a loss, where a gain on closing the option is included in the subsequent year. This rule applies to positions established after December 31, 1986.

The information above is from the booklet *Taxes and Investing: A Guide for the Individual Investor,* written by Ernst & Young LLP at the request of the option exchanges. It was published in January 2003 and is currently available in its entirety at www.cboe.com/resources/taxes.asp.

Twenty-Stock Covered Call Study*

Data

- Stock and option prices for expiration days were collected from the *Wall Street Journal* on microfiche.
- Stock prices for the Mondays following expiration and the end of the year were obtained from www.bigcharts.com.
- All prices were closing prices.
- Stock splits were included.
- Dividends were not included.

The Model

- Each stock was initially purchased in the largest number of round lots that $25,000 would buy. The actual amount spent became the initial investment in both the stock-alone and the covered-write scenarios.
- Commissions on the purchase and sale of all stocks and options were included using the rates from an online brokerage firm ($19.99 for up to 5,000 shares of stock and $20 + $1.75 per option contract).
- Excess cash from option premiums earned interest at 4 percent annually.
- If the option was in the money by any amount at the close on the Friday of expiration, the stock was assumed to be called away and then repurchased the following Monday at that day's closing price. Stock was always purchased in round lots, so if the price went up, fewer round lots may have been purchased following an assignment.
- When enough option premium had accumulated to buy another round lot of stock, the purchase was made.
- In the covered writing model, calls were written every month on all shares at the nearest out-of-the-money strike price, as long as they were worth at least $0.50 at the close of Monday's trading. Otherwise, no call was written that month. The stock was held (or repurchased if assigned) under all conditions.

*This study, conducted in 2002 by the authors is discussed in detail in Chapter 5.

Results for Individual Stocks by Year

ADVANCED MICRO DEVICES (AMD)   Initial Investment: $23,625

| Year | Stock Alone | | Covered Write | |
	Ending Value	Period Return	Ending Value	Period Return
6/88–	$12,938	-45%	$13,631	-42%
1989	$11,813	-9%	$13,416	-2%
1990	$7,313	-38%	$9,750	-27%
1991	$26,250	259%	$40,109	311%
1992	$27,000	3%	$42,233	5%
1993	$26,625	-1%	$36,879	-13%
1994	$37,125	39%	$43,507	18%
1995	$24,750	-33%	$28,021	-36%
1996	$38,625	56%	$40,449	44%
1997	$25,688	-33%	$43,045	6%
1998	$43,313	69%	$68,333	59%
1999	$43,500	0%	$71,430	5%
2000	$41,430	-5%	$70,757	-1%
2001	$47,580	15%	$77,065	9%
Annualized Return (6/88–12/01)		**5.3%**		**9.1%**

ASA   Initial Investment: $22,313

| Year | Stock Alone | | Covered Write | |
	Ending Value	Period Return	Ending Value	Period Return
6/88–	$19,000	-15%	$20,448	-8%
1989	$27,750	46%	$25,302	24%
1990	$23,438	-16%	$23,889	-6%
1991	$23,438	0%	$28,996	21%
1992	$15,938	-32%	$22,745	-22%
1993	$24,625	55%	$32,526	43%
1994	$22,438	-9%	$30,226	-7%
1995	$18,563	-17%	$27,578	-9%
1996	$17,375	-6%	$26,675	-3%
Annualized Return (6/88–12/96)		**-2.9%**		**2.1%**

CISCO SYSTEMS (CSCO)   Initial Investment: $22,500

| | Stock Alone | | Covered Write | |
Year	Ending Value	Period Return	Ending Value	Period Return
5/96–	$25,450	13%	$28,871	28%
1997	$33,825	33%	$33,363	16%
1998	$83,588	147%	$44,799	34%
1999	$192,713	131%	$86,602	93%
2000	$137,700	-29%	$81,597	-6%
2001	$65,196	-53%	$39,142	-52%
Annualized Return		**20.5%**		**10.2%**
(5/96–12/01)				

WALT DISNEY COMPANY (DIS)   Initial Investment: $23,660

| | Stock Alone | | Covered Write | |
Year	Ending Value	Period Return	Ending Value	Period Return
6/88–	$26,300	10%	$26,206	9%
1989	$44,800	70%	$33,486	28%
1990	$40,600	-9%	$32,891	-2%
1991	$45,800	13%	$35,762	9%
1992	$68,800	50%	$45,844	28%
1993	$68,200	-1%	$44,731	-2%
1994	$73,800	8%	$44,700	0%
1995	$94,400	28%	$58,543	31%
1996	$111,600	18%	$71,589	22%
1997	$158,400	42%	$92,852	30%
1998	$144,000	-9%	$85,562	-8%
1999	$140,400	-3%	$83,807	-2%
2000	$138,912	-1%	$87,694	5%
2001	$99,456	-28%	$68,700	-22%
Annualized Return		**11.1%**		**8.1%**
(6/88–12/01)				

EASTMAN KODAK COMPANY (EK)   Initial Investment: $21,563

| | Stock Alone | | Covered Write | |
Year	Ending Value	Period Return	Ending Value	Period Return
6/88–	$22,563	5%	$22,306	3%
1989	$20,563	-9%	$21,767	-2%
1990	$20,963	2%	$22,274	2%
1991	$24,125	15%	$22,552	1%
1992	$20,250	-16%	$19,105	-15%
1993	$28,000	38%	$24,902	30%
Annualized Return		**4.9%**		**2.7%**
(6/88–12/93)				

FEDEX CORPORATION (FDX)

Initial Investment: $24,750

| Year | Stock Alone | | Covered Write | |
	Ending Value	Period Return	Ending Value	Period Return
6/88–	$30,375	23%	$30,825	25%
1989	$27,450	-10%	$31,972	4%
1990	$20,325	-26%	$29,482	-8%
1991	$23,250	14%	$35,115	19%
1992	$32,700	41%	$41,054	17%
1993	$42,525	30%	$43,293	5%
1994	$36,150	-15%	$39,510	-9%
Annualized Return (6/88–12/94)		**6%**		**7.5%**

GENERAL MOTORS CORPORATION (GM)

Initial Investment: $23,063

| Year | Stock Alone | | Covered Write | |
	Ending Value	Period Return	Ending Value	Period Return
6/88–	$25,050	9%	$25,794	12%
1989	$25,350	1%	$25,800	0%
1990	$20,625	-19%	$23,778	-8%
1991	$17,325	-16%	$22,089	-7%
1992	$19,350	12%	$20,229	-8%
1993	$32,925	70%	$34,061	68%
1994	$25,350	-23%	$26,796	-21%
1995	$31,725	25%	$33,500	25%
1996	$33,450	5%	$34,008	2%
1997	$36,750	10%	$38,538	13%
1998	$42,975	17%	$41,340	7%
1999	$43,614	1%	$41,311	0%
Annualized Return (6/88–12/99)		**5.7%**		**5.2%**

HEWLETT-PACKARD COMPANY (HPQ)   Initial Investment: $23,063

	Stock Alone		Covered Write	
Year	Ending Value	Period Return	Ending Value	Period Return
6/88–	$21,174	-8%	$21,455	-7%
1989	$18,788	-11%	$22,160	3%
1990	$12,674	-33%	$17,054	-23%
1991	$22,665	79%	$26,427	55%
1992	$27,784	23%	$27,841	5%
1993	$31,413	13%	$32,785	18%
1994	$39,713	26%	$38,424	17%
1995	$66,603	68%	$55,691	45%
1996	$79,923	20%	$70,166	26%
1997	$97,912	23%	$89,979	28%
1998	$108,656	11%	$114,172	27%
1999	$180,921	67%	$154,150	35%
Annualized Return (6/88–12/99)	**19.5%**		**17.8%**	

IBM   Initial Investment: $22,626

	Stock alone		Covered Write	
Year	Ending Value	Period Return	Ending Value	Period Return
6/88–	$24,376	8%	$23,961	6%
1989	$18,826	-23%	$21,664	-10%
1990	$22,601	20%	$25,401	17%
1991	$17,801	-21%	$19,548	-23%
1992	$10,075	-43%	$13,420	-31%
1993	$11,300	12%	$15,248	14%
1994	$14,701	30%	$17,079	12%
1995	$18,351	25%	$18,692	9%
1996	$30,301	65%	$21,148	13%
1997	$41,302	36%	$27,289	29%
1998	$73,903	79%	$33,960	24%
1999	$86,304	17%	$36,469	7%
2000	$68,003	-21%	$33,593	-8%
2001	$96,772	42%	$39,197	17%
Annualized Return (6/88–12/01)	**11.3%**		**4.1%**	

INTEL CORPORATION (INTC)

Initial Investment: $25,000

Year	Stock Alone Ending Value	Period Return	Covered Write Ending Value	Period Return
6/88–	$19,000	-24%	$21,912	-12%
1989	$27,600	45%	$29,535	35%
1990	$30,800	12%	$33,844	15%
1991	$39,200	27%	$41,552	23%
1992	$69,600	78%	$49,311	19%
1993	$99,200	43%	$61,740	25%
1994	$102,200	3%	$60,600	-2%
1995	$181,600	78%	$92,639	53%
1996	$418,400	130%	$151,463	63%
1997	$458,800	10%	$181,333	20%
1998	$759,200	65%	$214,048	18%
1999	$1,068,800	41%	$257,636	20%
2000	$774,400	-28%	$174,185	-32%
2001	$805,120	4%	$199,853	15%
Annualized Return (6/88–12/01)		**29.1%**		**16.5%**

MCDONALD'S CORPORATION (MCD)

Initial Investment: $22,375

Year	Stock Alone Ending Value	Period Return	Covered Write Ending Value	Period Return
6/88–	$24,063	8%	$24,208	8%
1989	$17,250	-28%	$18,369	-24%
1990	$14,563	-16%	$16,565	-10%
1991	$19,000	30%	$20,589	24%
1992	$24,375	28%	$27,701	35%
1993	$28,500	17%	$33,195	20%
1994	$29,250	3%	$34,517	4%
1995	$45,125	54%	$51,980	51%
1996	$45,375	1%	$51,538	-1%
1997	$47,250	4%	$57,063	11%
1998	$76,810	63%	$79,764	40%
1999	$80,620	5%	$88,690	11%
Annualized Return (6/88–12/99)		**11.7%**		**12.6%**

3M COMPANY (MMM)

Initial Investment: $25,050

| | Stock Alone | | Covered Write | |
Year	Ending Value	Period Return	Ending Value	Period Return
6/88–	$24,800	-1%	$24,934	0%
1989	$31,850	28%	$32,961	32%
1990	$34,300	8%	$38,110	16%
1991	$38,100	11%	$44,163	16%
1992	$40,250	6%	$49,543	12%
1993	$43,500	8%	$54,076	9%
1994	$42,900	-1%	$53,770	-1%
1995	$53,100	24%	$66,939	24%
Annualized Return (6/88–12/95)		**10.5%**		**14.0%**

PHILIP MORRIS COMPANIES (MO)

Initial Investment: $25,763

| | Stock Alone | | Covered Write | |
Year	Ending Value	Period Return	Ending Value	Period Return
6/88–	$30,563	19%	$27,163	5%
1989	$49,950	63%	$38,649	42%
1990	$62,100	24%	$44,891	16%
1991	$94,800	53%	$58,012	29%
1992	$92,400	-3%	$58,650	1%
1993	$66,900	-28%	$48,936	-17%
1994	$69,000	3%	$51,616	5%
1995	$108,600	57%	$75,265	46%
1996	$135,600	25%	$89,082	18%
1997	$162,227	20%	$124,315	40%
1998	$192,600	19%	$147,493	19%
1999	$82,800	-57%	$67,026	-55%
2000	$158,400	91%	$81,561	22%
2001	$165,060	4%	$93,496	15%
Annualized Return (6/88–12/01)		**14.7%**		**0.0%**

MERCK & COMPANY (MRK)

Initial Investment: $22,100

Year	Stock Alone Ending Value	Period Return	Covered Write Ending Value	Period Return
6/88–	$23,100	5%	$24,445	11%
1989	$31,000	34%	$31,263	28%
1990	$35,950	16%	$32,942	5%
1991	$66,600	85%	$47,212	43%
1992	$52,200	-22%	$44,093	-7%
1993	$41,250	-21%	$35,952	-18%
1994	$45,750	11%	$38,449	7%
1995	$78,900	72%	$58,770	53%
1996	$95,550	21%	$74,473	27%
1997	$128,100	34%	$88,453	19%
1998	$177,300	38%	$120,243	36%
1999	$161,400	-9%	$131,868	10%
2000	$224,712	39%	$163,507	24%
2001	$141,120	-37%	$127,901	-22%
Annualized Return (6/88–12/01)		**14.6%**		**13.8%**

MICROSOFT CORPORATION (MFST)

Initial Investment: $23,700

Year	Stock Alone Ending Value	Period Return	Covered Write Ending Value	Period Return
6/88–	$21,300	-10%	$22,595	-5%
1989	$34,800	63%	$26,120	16%
1990	$60,200	73%	$36,971	42%
1991	$133,500	122%	$64,769	75%
1992	$153,675	15%	$72,217	12%
1993	$145,125	-6%	$76,261	6%
1994	$220,050	52%	$102,434	34%
1995	$315,900	44%	$138,307	35%
1996	$594,900	88%	$256,939	86%
1997	$937,800	58%	$431,976	68%
1998	$1,998,000	113%	$590,287	37%
1999	$3,351,600	68%	$786,984	33%
2000	$1,252,800	-63%	$398,669	-49%
2001	$1,908,576	52%	$513,292	29%
Annualized Return (6/88–12/01)		**38.2%**		**25.4%**

ORACLE CORPORATION (ORCL)   Initial Investment: $23,975

| | Stock Alone | | Covered Write | |
Year	Ending Value	Period Return	Ending Value	Period Return
6/88–	$27,300	14%	$29,802	24%
1989	$65,450	140%	$53,325	79%
1990	$22,050	-66%	$16,622	-69%
1991	$40,600	84%	$29,146	75%
1992	$79,450	96%	$46,048	58%
1993	$161,000	103%	$69,758	51%
1994	$248,500	54%	$120,938	73%
1995	$355,950	43%	$183,040	51%
1996	$519,750	46%	$282,464	54%
1997	$422,888	-19%	$247,059	-13%
1998	$815,063	93%	$379,333	54%
1999	$3,161,025	288%	$573,199	51%
2000	$3,295,404	4%	$599,715	5%
2001	$1,566,054	-52%	$429,213	-28%
Annualized Return (6/88–12/01)		**36.0%**		**23.7%**

PHILLIPS PETROLEUM (P)   Initial Investment: $24,325

| | Stock Alone | | Covered Write | |
Year	Ending Value	Period Return	Ending Value	Period Return
6/88–	$27,300	12%	$28,933	19%
1989	$35,350	29%	$34,720	20%
1990	$36,575	3%	$36,689	6%
1991	$33,600	-8%	$32,046	-13%
1992	$35,175	5%	$34,671	8%
–7/93	$40,250	14%	$40,989	18%
Annualized Return (6/88–7/93)		**10.4%**		**10.8%**

TOYS "R" US (TOY)

Initial Investment: $21,825

	Stock Alone		Covered Write	
Year	Ending Value	Period Return	Ending Value	Period Return
6/88–	$22,275	2%	$22,910	5%
1989	$32,288	45%	$31,552	38%
1990	$30,375	-6%	$29,671	-6%
1991	$43,538	43%	$47,909	61%
1992	$54,169	24%	$56,497	18%
1993	$55,181	2%	$57,683	2%
1994	$41,175	-25%	$46,283	-20%
1995	$29,363	-29%	$34,038	-26%
1996	$40,331	37%	$48,709	43%
Annualized Return (6/88–12/96)		7.5%		9.9%

WAL-MART STORES (WMT)

Initial Investment: $23,400

	Stock Alone		Covered Write	
Year	Ending Value	Period Return	Ending Value	Period Return
6/88–	$25,100	7%	$26,793	14%
1989	$35,900	43%	$35,531	33%
1990	$48,400	35%	$50,498	42%
1991	$94,200	95%	$90,635	79%
1992	$101,800	8%	$109,945	21%
1993	$80,000	-21%	$90,005	-18%
1994	$68,000	-15%	$71,653	-20%
1995	$71,600	5%	$76,916	7%
Annualized Return (6/88–12/95)		16.1%		17.2%

SUN MICROSYSTEMS (SUNW)   Initial Investment: $23,888

Year	Stock Alone		Covered Write	
	Ending Value	Period Return	Ending Value	Period Return
6/88–	$11,638	-51%	$13,347	-44%
1989	$24,150	108%	$26,317	97%
1990	$29,925	24%	$32,557	24%
1991	$39,725	33%	$51,735	59%
1992	$47,075	19%	$65,408	26%
1993	$40,775	-13%	$70,459	8%
1994	$49,700	22%	$81,725	16%
1995	$127,750	157%	$153,707	88%
1996	$144,200	13%	$212,332	38%
1997	$227,500	58%	$284,048	34%
1998	$479,500	111%	$410,251	44%
1999	$1,733,200	261%	$857,006	109%
2000	$1,249,024	-28%	$695,767	-19%
2001	$553,280	-56%	$509,347	-27%
Annualized Return (6/88–12/01)		**26.0%**		**25.3%**

Bibliography

Ansbacher, Max. *The New Options Market*. New York: John Wiley & Sons, Inc., 2000.

Chicago Board Options Exchange Constitution and Rules. Chicago: CCH Incorporated, 2001.

Friedentag, Harvey C. *Stocks for Options Trading: Low-Risk, Low-Stress Strategies for Selling Stock Options Profitably*. Boca Raton: CRC Press LLC, 2000.

Gross, Leroy. *The Conservative Investor's Guide to Trading Options*. New York: John Wiley & Sons, Inc., 1999.

Hirsch, Yale and Jeffrey A. Hirsch. *Stock Trader's Almanac 2002*. New Jersey: The Hirsch Organization Inc., 2001.

McMillan, Lawrence G. *Options as a Strategic Investment*. New York: Prentice Hall Press, 2002.

Options Institute, The, ed. *Options: Essential Concepts and Trading Strategies*. New York: McGraw-Hill, 1999.

Thomsett, Michael C. *Getting Started in Options*. New York: John Wiley & Sons, Inc., 2001.

Williams, Michael S. and Amy Hoffman. *Fundamentals of the Option Market*. New York: McGraw-Hill, 2001.

Glossary

adjustment. An alteration of the terms of the option contract that may be undertaken by a joint panel of the option exchange and the OCC when certain events affecting an underlying security occur, such as a stock split, merger, or spin-off. The object is to ensure that both holders and writers of the option have essentially the same position after the event as they did before. When an option has been adjusted from standard terms, it receives a different symbol.

American style. Options that can be exercised at any time before expiration. Equity options on individual stocks all trade American style.

arbitrage. Profiting from the disparities in price of equivalent securities traded simultaneously in more than one market.

assignment. The action that the OCC and your broker take in selecting option sellers to fulfill the obligation stipulated by the option they sold. When call writers receive assignment notices from their brokers, they are selling the underlying stock at the designated strike price.

at the money. Describes an option that has a strike price equal or close to the current price of the underlying stock. Example: A GHI call option with a strike of 30 is at the money when the stock is trading at $30 or $29.75.

Black-Scholes formula. A formula for calculating the theoretical premium or value of an option. The factors considered in this formula include the price of the underlying stock, the strike price of the option, the amount of time left until expiration, the volatility of the underlying stock, any dividends paid, and the current interest rate.

buyer (or holder). The party in an option transaction who is long the contract.

buy-write approach (also total-return approach). Using continuous covered call writing as a primary investment strategy to generate an attractive total return, with a portfolio specifically designed for that purpose.

BuyWrite Index (BXM). A new benchmark created by the CBOE that emulates an ongoing covered call writing strategy on the Standard & Poor's 500 Index.

call-on-call covered write. Covering calls with other options. Also called *bull calendar call spreads* or *diagonal spreads.*

call option. A contract representing the right, for a specified term, to buy a specified security at a specified price.

cash value. *See* **intrinsic value.**

Chicago Board Options Exchange (CBOE). The largest U.S. market for trading options.

class. All the options of the same type that have the same underlying security.

For example, all the call options on Microsoft stock are part of the same class, regardless of strike price or expiration.

closing transaction. A trade in which an existing position in an option is offset by the purchase (if the existing position is short) or the sale (if the existing position is long) of the identical security.

contract size. The number of shares of the underlying security that must be delivered when an option holder exercises the contract. The standard contract size of an equity option is 100 shares.

conversion. A type of arbitrage that involves purchasing a stock and then buying a put and selling a call on it, with both options having the same strike price and expiration.

covered. Describes a short option position that is secured by a long position in the underlying stock (or a security that is convertible into the stock) large enough to fulfill an assignment.

covered call writing. Selling call options on stock whose shares you hold or buy simultaneously.

deliverable. The security that must be delivered if an option holder exercises the contract.

derivative security. A financial instrument whose value is based on that of another security or benchmark.

designated primary market maker (DPM). A floor trader on the Chicago Board Options Exchange whose function, much like that of a specialist on the New York Stock Exchange, is to maintain an orderly two-sided market for a specific security.

dividend. A cash distribution that a company makes to shareholders from its earnings.

downside. A disadvantageous aspect of a transaction.

equity options. Options whose underlying security is stock.

European style. Options that can be exercised only at expiration. Index options trade European style.

exchange-traded funds (ETFs). Securities that track an index's performance, as an index mutual fund does, but that trade on an exchange, like stock.

exercise. The action that option holders take when they notify their brokers of their intent to invoke the right, represented by their option, to buy (or sell) the underlying security at the strike price.

exercise price. *See* **strike price.**

expiration date. The date when the terms of an option contract terminate.

extrinsic value. *See* **time value.**

holder. *See* **buyer.**

in the money. Describes a *call* option whose strike price is *below* the current price of the underlying stock or a *put* with a strike *above* the current price. Example: When ABC stock is trading at $43, call options with strike prices of 40, 35, and 30 are all in the money.

premium. The price of an option or, more accurately, the money you pay or receive when you buy or sell it. In the case of a standard equity option, this equals the share price times 100.

put option. A contract representing the right for a specified time to sell a specified security at a specified price.

ratio writing. Selling more than one call option per 100 shares of stock held.

return based on a net debit. A method of calculating the potential return of a covered call position using as the initial investment the difference between the proceeds from writing the call option and the cost of buying the stock.

return unchanged (RU, also static or flat return). The potential return on a covered call position if, at option expiration, the underlying stock is trading at its purchase price. RU equals the option premium received divided by the initial investment.

returned if exercised (RIE, also return if assigned or if called). The potential gain on a covered call position if the writer is assigned on the call option. RIE equals the potential gain in the stock (up to the strike price) plus the option premium received, divided by the initial investment.

reversal. A type of arbitrage that involves short stock and put positions and a long call position, with both options having the same strike and expiration.

rolling down. Closing the short option position in a covered call and substituting one with a lower strike price.

rolling out. Closing the short option position in a covered call and substituting one with a more distant expiration.

rolling up. Closing the short option position in a covered call and substituting one with a higher strike price.

seller (also writer). The party in an option transaction who is short the contract.

series. All the options in the same class that also have the same strike price and expiration date.

settlement. The process of delivering an underlying security (or other stipulated interest) as a result of an option exercise.

short selling stock. Selling stock that you borrow, hoping to replace the shares with others that you purchase in the market later at a lower price.

specialist. An exchange member who is responsible for maintaining an orderly market in a specific group of securities by trading from his or her own account when there are no external buyers or sellers to take the other side of an order.

spread order. A single order that involves both a purchase and a sale of options of the same type on the same stock for a specified net price. Covered writers frequently use spread orders to roll their option positions.

intrinsic value. One of the two components, with time value, of an
price. It equals the amount, if any, by which an option is in the
Example: An ABC call option with a strike of 40 has $3 of intrins
if ABC is trading at $43. The same option has zero intrinsic value
is trading anywhere below $40.

limit order. An order to buy or sell securities that specifies a price th
be met or bettered for execution to occur.

liquidity. The degree of ease with which a security may be trac
indication of liquidity is the daily trading volume in the security

listed options. Options that are formally traded on a recognized exch

long. Term used to describe the position of the buyer of a security.

long-term equity anticipation securities (LEAPS). Options wit
greater than nine months.

margin account. A type of brokerage account in which you can borrc
from your broker with which to buy investments.

naked (also uncovered). Refers to a short option position that is not
by shares of the underlying stock.

net credit. The result of a combination transaction consisting of a sa
security and a purchase of another in which the proceeds from
are greater than the cost of the purchase.

net debit. The result of a combination transaction consisting of a sa
security and a purchase of another in which the proceeds from
are smaller than the cost of the purchase.

net price. The cost of a combination transaction involving a purcha
security and a sale of another.

open interest. The number of contracts remaining unclosed for a ʝ
option. In conjunction with the daily volume of contracts tra
figure provides an indication of the option's liquidity.

opening rotation. A procedure used by option exchanges at the beg
the trading day to ensure an orderly market.

opening transaction. Transaction initiating a position.

option. A contract representing the right, for a specified term, to bu
specified security at a specified price.

option chain (also option strings or montages). A basic summary
lists all the available options on a particular stock.

Options Clearing Corp. (OCC). An independent entity that acts as
and guarantor for all listed option contracts.

out of the money. Describes a *call* option whose strike price is
current price of the underlying stock or a *put* with a strike
current price. Example: When ABC stock is trading at $43, ca
with strike prices of 45, 50, and 55 are all out of the money.

parity. Term applied to an in-the-money option that trades exa
intrinsic value.

strike price (also exercise price). The price at which an option's underlying security of can be purchased, in the case of a call, or sold, for a put, by the contract holder.

time value (also extrinsic value). One of the two components, with intrinsic value, of an option's price. It equals the amount, if any, by which an option's price exceeds its intrinsic value. Example: If ABC is trading at $43, an ABC call option with a strike of 40 that is trading at 5 has $2 of time value. The same option has zero time value if it is trading at 3.

total-return approach. *See* **buy-write approach.**

uncovered. *See* **naked.**

underlying. The security that an option gives its holder the right to buy or sell.

volatility. A statistical measure of how much a security has moved (or potentially *can* move) in a given amount of time, either up or down, usually expressed as the standard deviation of daily change in price over a specified period.

volatility skew. The different volatilities implied by the different options on a given stock.

writer. *See* **seller.**

Index

About Bloomberg

Bloomberg L.P., founded in 1981, is a global information services, news, and media company. Headquartered in New York, the company has nine sales offices, two data centers, and 87 news bureaus worldwide.

Bloomberg, serving customers in 126 countries around the world, holds a unique position within the financial services industry by providing an unparalleled range of features in a single package known as the BLOOMBERG PROFESSIONAL® service. By addressing the demand for investment performance and efficiency through an exceptional combination of information, analytic, electronic trading, and Straight Through Processing tools, Bloomberg has built a worldwide customer base of corporations, issuers, financial intermediaries, and institutional investors.

BLOOMBERG NEWS®, founded in 1990, provides stories and columns on business, general news, politics, and sports to leading newspapers and magazines throughout the world. BLOOMBERG TELEVISION®, a 24-hour business and financial news network, is produced and distributed globally in seven different languages. BLOOMBERG RADIO^{SM} is an international radio network anchored by flagship station BLOOMBERG® 1130 (WBBR-AM) in New York.

In addition to the BLOOMBERG PRESS® line of books, Bloomberg publishes *BLOOMBERG MARKETS™* and *BLOOMBERG WEALTH MANAGER®*. To learn more about Bloomberg, call a sales representative at:

Frankfurt:	49-69-92041-280	São Paulo:	5511-3048-4506
Hong Kong:	852-2977-6900	Singapore:	65-6212-1100
London:	44-20-7330-7500	Sydney:	612-9777-8686
New York:	1-212-318-2200	Tokyo:	813-3201-8910
San Francisco:	1-415-912-2970		

For in-depth market information and news, visit the Bloomberg website at **www.bloomberg.com**, which draws from the news and power of the BLOOMBERG PROFESSIONAL® service and Bloomberg's host of media products to provide high-quality news and information in multiple languages on stocks, bonds, currencies, and commodities.

About the Authors

Richard Lehman is the principal of Lehman Investment Advisors, an advisory firm specializing in option writing strategies. The firm offers money management and an online advisory service at www.covered writer.com. Mr. Lehman has more than twenty-five years experience as a Wall Street derivatives specialist, having held executive positions involving options marketing and sales activities at EF Hutton, Thomson McKinnon Securities, and the boutique investment firm First Saxonia Securities. While at Hutton, he marketed options to 1,000 sales reps in the Atlantic region along with managing retail investment accounts for option clients, and was named "top broker" in an independent national option trading championship. As a marketing executive for the New York Stock Exchange in the early 1980s, he explored plans for trading of options and futures on the NYSE and edited and produced for that organization a 200-page market research study on public attitudes toward investing. The author holds a B.S. degree in management engineering from Rensselaer Polytechnic Institute and an M.B.A. in marketing from the State University of New York at Albany. He lives in the San Francisco Bay Area.

Lawrence G. McMillan is recognized as an options trading industry expert, and serious investors have relied on his insights, observations, and recommendations for years. As the president of McMillan Analysis Corporation, he edits and publishes *The Option Strategist*, a derivative products newsletter covering equity, index, and futures options, and also runs "Daily Volume Alerts." This unique daily fax service selects short-term stock trades by looking for unusual increases in equity option volume. In addition, he has a short-term stock and option trading website at www.option-strategist.com, and he speaks regularly on option strategies at traders conferences and seminars throughout North America and Europe. Mr. McMillan is the author of *Options as a Strategic Investment*, the best-selling work on stock and index options strategies which has sold over 200,000 copies, and also *McMillan on Options*. Prior to opening his own firm, McMillan worked for Thomson McKinnon Securities, where he was in charge of equity arbitrage, and also Prudential-Bache Securities, where he was in charge of the proprietary option trading. Mr. McMillan holds a B.S. degree in mathematics from Purdue University and an M.S. in applied mathematics and computer science from the University of Colorado.